VENICE
CONDENSED

D0973334

Damien Simonis

LONELY PLANET PUBLICATIONS
Melbourne • Oakland • London • Paris

contents

Venice Condensed
1st edition – June 2002

Published by
Lonely Planet Publications Pty Ltd
ABN 36 005 607 983
90 Maribyrnong St, Footscray, Vic 3011, Australia
www.lonelyplanet.com or AOL keyword: lp

Lonely Planet offices
Australia Locked Bag 1, Footscray, Vic 3011
☎ 613 8379 8000 fax 613 8379 8111
e talk2us@lonelyplanet.com.au
USA 150 Linden St, Oakland, CA 94607
☎ 510 893 8555 Toll Free: 800 275 8555
fax 510 893 8572
e info@lonelyplanet.com
UK 10a Spring Place, London NW5 3BH
☎ 020 7428 4800 fax 020 7428 4828
e go@lonelyplanet.co.uk
France 1 rue du Dahomey, 75011 Paris
☎ 01 55 25 33 00 fax 01 55 25 33 01
e bip@lonelyplanet.fr
www.lonelyplanet.fr

Design Annika Roojun Maps Charles Rawlings-Way,
Jolyon Philcox & Rachel Beattie Editing Sally Schafer
Proofing Emma Sangster Cover Jenny Jones Publishing
Manager Diana Saad Thanks to Amanda Canning,
Bridget Blair, Gabrielle Green, Gerald Walker, Imogen
Franks, James Hardy, Kerrie Williams, Lachlan Ross,
Lou Byrnes, Nikki Anderson, Paul Piaia, Quentin Frayne
& Rowan McKinnon

Photographs
Many of the images in this guide are available for
licensing from Lonely Planet Images:
www.lonelyplanetimages.com
Images also used with kind permission of APL/Corbis.

Front cover photographs
Top Ponte di Rialto
(Jon Davison)
Bottom Detail of Palazzo Bembo
(Damien Simonis)

ISBN 1 74059 317 0

Text & maps © Lonely Planet Publications Pty Ltd 2002
Grateful acknowledgment is made for reproduction
permission of transit map: © ACTV: Venice Vaporetto
Map 2002
Photos © photographers as indicated 2002
Printed by The Bookmaker International Ltd
Printed in China

how to use this book

SYMBOLS

- ✉ address
- ☎ telephone number
- 🚉 nearest vaporetto/traghetto stop
- 🚆 nearest train station
- 🚌 nearest bus route
- ◷ opening hours
- ⓘ tourist information
- ⑤ cost, admission charge
- e email/website address
- ♿ wheelchair access
- ♣ child-friendly
- ✗ on-site or nearby eatery
- V good vegetarian selection

COLOUR-CODING

Each chapter has a different colour code which is reflected on the maps for quick reference (eg all Highlights are bright yellow on the maps).

MAPS

The fold-out maps inside the front and back covers are numbered from 1 to 5. All sights and venues in the text have map references which indicate where to find them on the maps; eg (3, G12) means Map 3, grid reference G12. Although each item is not pin-pointed on the maps, the street address is always indicated.

PRICES

The price gradings (eg €10/5) given in this book usually indicate adult/concession admission charges to a venue. Concession prices can include senior and student discounts.

AUTHOR AUTHOR !

Damien Simonis

Since his first trip to Venice, Damien has been unable to shake the spell of this strange and bewitching city.

Damien does not spend a lot of time in one place, with bases in London and Barcelona and a steady diet of the road. He has written more than a dozen guidebooks for Lonely Planet and other publishers, and written and shot for publications in Australia, the UK and North America.

To Irina Fraguia, who went well out of her way to help me out, *grazie infinite*. Thanks also (in no particular order) to: Michela Scibilia, Roberta Guarnieri, Bernhard Klein, Federica Centulani, Caterina De Cesero, Susanne Sagner, Lucialda Lombardi, Alberto Stassi, Anna Cerutti, Daniela Antongiovanni, Sergio Bosio and Paola Brussa.

READER FEEDBACK

Things change – prices go up, schedules change, good places go bad and bad places improve or go bankrupt. So, if you find things better or worse, recently opened or long since closed, please tell us and help make the next edition even more accurate. Send all correspondence to the Lonely Planet office closest to you (listed on p. 2) or visit www.lonelyplanet.com/feedback.

facts about venice

Decaying, awash in winter, drained of its people, the unique city-on-the-water appears moribund. Yet Venice, like the old courtesan it is frequently compared with, remains unperturbed. And the courtesan has lost none of her power to bewitch. Of all the great Italian cities, Venice remains the most beguiling.

The lagoon city, which rose to become Europe's most powerful merchant empire and was known to all as La Serenissima, The Most Serene, captivates merely by its appearance. One of the simplest and most inexhaustible joys is to wander the narrow canalside lanes, cross its innumerable little bridges, and get lost in its labyrinth. In no other city in the world can it be said that the main form of transport is your own two feet…followed by boat! Listen – there are no cars, and some people choose to live here for that reason alone.

Venice is a festival of art and architecture. It is High Renaissance. Tiepolo, Tintoretto, Veronese and Titian head a roll call too long to contemplate. The very city is a work of art, an extraordinary catalogue ranging from Romanesque and Veneto-Byzantine to Gothic and the rational magnificence of Palladio. It is a crucible of cultures, a meeting point of East and West.

Tourists flock to it, tacky restaurants and souvenir stands abound and the gondola ride has become a cheesy obligation. But you need little imagination, only the initiative to get off the main tourist thoroughfares, to plunge into the romance and melancholy of it all, as if cradled by the lapping of the lagoon's waters.

One man's romantic ride is another's daily commute.

HISTORY
A Swampy Refuge

Venice, it is claimed, was founded on a string of straggly islets in the Venetian lagoon in AD421. A more telling date is 452, when Attila the Hun and his marauding armies crashed into northeastern Italy (aka the Veneto) and sent its inhabitants fleeing to the lagoon for safety. It was a pattern that would be repeated and in 726 the island communities came together under their first *doge* (duke). Most of those on the islands lived in miserable malarial conditions, but they were becoming hardy fishermen and sea traders. No-one could navigate the lagoon like them. By the 9th century their administrative centre had become the islands around Rivo Alto (today Rialto). Over the succeeding centuries, by reclaiming land and creating artificial islands on beds of wooden pylons, the Rivo Alto took on the present shape of Venice, or Venezia as it would be known from the 12th century on.

The Lion's Tale

Wherever Venice's law held sway, the Republic's ensign, the Lion of St Mark, fluttered. A stirring mascot no doubt, and in the mists of early medieval Venetian history an elaborate tale emerged to explain how it came to represent Venice. An angel allegedly told the Evangelist St Mark (represented in Christian iconography by the lion) that he would one day rest in the lagoon. In AD828, in fulfilment of the prophecy, Venetian merchants smuggled the saint's corpse out of Alexandria, Egypt. Hurrah! Now Venice could claim one of the big guns as its patron saint.

Damien Simonis

Venice's mascot: the Lion of St Mark

Venice Victorious

By 1095, when the First Crusade was called to liberate the Holy Lands from the Muslims, Venice had consolidated itself as an oligarchic republic under an elected doge. The electoral system and echelons of government were immensely complicated, but essentially power was concentrated in the hands of a potent elite.

Much of that power came from the extraordinarily successful trading empire that the Venetians had established. Demonstrating the extent to which the lagoon city danced to its own tune, Venice ignored the sensibilities of other Christian powers and courted favours with Muslim centres from Córdoba to Damascus in the pursuit of trade.

The city's wily ambassadors attempted to keep sweet as many parties as possible, which wasn't always easy. The Crusades put Venice on the spot. It participated only minimally, but in so doing weakened its ties with the Byzantine Empire. The situation reached its lowest ebb when Venice convinced crusading allies to sack Constantinople in 1203. Relations with Muslim powers waxed and waned. Other European powers and the pope remained wary of Venice.

Rival Italian sea powers, especially Genoa, were a great source of anguish, and in 1380 the Genoese even attempted a siege of Venice. The great wave of plague in 1348 had decimated the city too. Yet through it all the Venetians continued to extend their power.

When Constantinople fell to the Ottoman Turks in 1453 (signalling the demise of the Byzantine Empire, of which in the early days Venice had been little more than a peripheral appendage) Venice had reached the apogee of its power.

The city ruled the Adriatic as its own lake – all trading vessels using it had to pay customs in Venice. The Venetians controlled much of the Dalmatian coast, along with a series of strategic islands (including Crete) throughout Greece. It had acquired a considerable land empire, stretching from Friuli in the east to Bergamo in the west. Trade was brisk. Through its network of depots across the Near East and as far off as the Black Sea, Venice continued to be a cardinal link between the East and Europe. And by now Venice's Arsenale, a fortified shipyard that churned out fighting and merchant vessels on an industrial scale, was at its peak.

Decline

It couldn't last. By the end of the 15th century the Turks had become clearly hostile and begun the long process of nibbling away at the city's possessions. Venice could do little while the remainder of the West remained disunited. Indeed, Venice found itself on occasion fighting the Turks *and* Western powers.

> ### Denunciation & Death
>
> In the wake of an unsuccessful revolt in 1310, Venice set up the Consiglio dei Dieci (Council of Ten), which became one of the most powerful and feared branches of an already complex governmental system. This early CIA received anonymous hand-written tip-offs in the *bocche di denunce*, glorified letter boxes in the Doge's Palace. When the council found a traitor or other miscreant, justice was swift and quiet. Bodies simply turned up floating in canals or strung up in St Mark's Square. The Republic had a formidable reputation and its spies ranged across Europe in search of La Serenissima's enemies.

Damien Simonis

Keep your head down in St Mark's!

The rounding of the Cape of Good Hope by the Portuguese Vasco da Gama at the end of the 15th century boded ill for Venetian trade, as did the rise of vigorous nation states such as England and France. The fall of Crete to the Turks in the late 17th century was a further hammer blow.

Venice clung to its mainland possessions and managed to avoid trouble for another century. But the city lost its appetite for struggle. With trade much reduced and the coffers empty, the noble class sank. Many grandees were destitute. Those who could afford to, played. In the 18th century Venice came to be known throughout Europe as a party town. Carnevale lasted as long as two months, casinos did a roaring trade and Venetian prostitutes of every class were rarely short of clients.

Napoleon, Austria & Unity

The end could not have been more ignominious. Napoleon marched into northern Italy in the late 1790s in pursuit of Austrian forces. On the way he decided to take Venice. After procrastinating and attempting every ruse they could think of, the Venetians simply surrendered. Napoleon swaggered into St Mark's Square (Piazza San Marco), 'Europe's finest drawing room', without firing a shot. The city became a marginal pawn on a much broader chessboard. Napoleon handed it to Austria in 1798, incorporated it into his puppet Kingdom of Italy in 1805 and finally lost everything in 1815. By treaty Venice went back to the Austrians, who remained in control until 1866, the year in which Venice, after several rebellions, joined the newly formed and independent Kingdom of Italy.

The last decades of the 19th century saw port and trade life pick up again. Industrial activity on Giudecca and the mainland got under way and the beginnings of tourism presaged the future. Under Mussolini's rule, the road bridge between Venice and the mainland was built.

Venice Today

After WWII, industrial expansion on the mainland continued with the creation of a huge petrochemical complex that might have been good for the economy, but has proved noxious for the lagoon. In 1966 record floods devastated the city and it became clear that it might one day be engulfed. People began to vote with their feet – the population today is less than half of what it was in the 1950s. International events such as the art Biennale and the annual cinema festival on the Lido, along with its romantic reputation, keep Venice in the spotlight, but more than three decades after 1966 little has been done to protect the city from the sea that once was its greatest defence.

Stripy poles for mooring boats

Damien Simons

ENVIRONMENT

The lagoon from which Venice rises and which for centuries formed its most effective line of defence is under attack.

Formed 6000 years ago by the meeting of the sea with freshwater streams running off Alpine rivers, the lagoon is like a shallow dish, criss-crossed by numerous navigable channels (some natural, others man-made). More than 40 islands dot the lagoon, whose seaward side is protected by a 50km arc of long narrow islands (including the Lido) that stem the inward flow of the Adriatic.

From the 16th century, human intervention was stepped up with the diversion of freshwater streams away from the lagoon to reduce sediment build-up. The 20th century brought more drastic changes. In the 1960s a deep channel was dug through to the petrochemical complex in Porto Marghera. This allows in supertankers and too much sea water. The industrial plants spew toxic waste into the lagoon. More waste is tipped in from Venice and other islands and mainland towns. Clean-up plans were finally drawn up in 2001.

The survival of the lagoon depends on the regulated ebb and flow of sea water and the inflow of fresh water and sediment. Sea tides flush out the lagoon and thus create a sustainable environment for flora and sea life. Some sediment is important for the creation of natural sandbanks (*velme* and *barene*), which in turn help regulate tides. Dragnet clam fishing has damaged the lagoon floor and further threatened flora and fish.

Flooding in Venice has always been a problem. In winter, high Adriatic tides push into the lagoon and inundate the city. In 1966 disastrous flooding set alarm bells ringing around the world. They still ring, but little has been done to halt the problem. In addition to the rising sea level, the city is sinking (a conservative estimate is 14cm in the 20th century) due to subsidence.

The controversial Mose project to fit the lagoon's sea entrances with mobile barriers, which would rise when tides were dangerously high, was approved in late 2001 after more than 20 years on the drawing board. The project, if it really does get under way, will take at least eight years to complete.

Siren Call

Acqua alta (high water) officially begins at 0.8m above average sea level. Sixteen air-raid sirens around the city go off if it is expected to hit 1.1m. Over 1.2m you can be in trouble, as even the walkways set up in strategic parts of town are no use. At 1.4m a state of emergency would be declared. The November 1966 flood level was 1.94m.

Damien Simons

Tidal tranquillity on the Grand Canal

ORIENTATION

The city of Venice includes the fish-shaped Venice proper, the islands of the lagoon, and mainland territory (including Mestre). Marco Polo airport lies east of Mestre, 12km from Venice. The train station, Stazione di Santa

Lucia, is in the northwest of town, at the end of the Ponte della Libertà – the bridge from the mainland. The bus station is on the opposite (southern) side of the Grand Canal (Canal Grande) in Piazzale Roma.

Venice proper, the *centro storico* (historic centre), is compact. It is built on 117 small islands and bisected by the Grand Canal. Through it run 150 canals crossed by 409 bridges, of which only three span the Grand Canal.

St Mark's doorstep: Bacino di San Marco

The city is divided into six quarters *(sestieri)*: Cannaregio, Castello, San Marco, Dorsoduro, San Polo and Santa Croce. These divisions date from 1171. In 1841 the Austrians devised a curious numbering system. Addresses in each district were numbered from 1 to whatever (1-2344 in Santa Croce, 1-6827 in Castello). Postal addresses rarely have street names. Send a letter to San Marco 3456 and the postie will know where to go.

GOVERNMENT & POLITICS

Venice is the capital of the region known as the Veneto (one of 20 in Italy), which extends west to Verona and Lake Garda and north into the Alps. The Veneto is subdivided into seven provinces, of which the area around Venice – Venezia – is one.

Since 1927, the *comune*, or municipality, of Venice has comprised the islands of the lagoon (including Murano, Burano, Torcello, the Lido and Pellestrina), as well as Mestre, Porto Marghera and Chioggia and a few other centres on the mainland. Locals divide the lot into three areas: *terraferma* (mainland), centro storico (Venice proper, including Giudecca) and the *estuario* (the remaining islands). The whole is divided into 13 *quartieri*, although traditionally Venice itself is made up of six sestieri (see Orientation).

Did You Know?
- **Population (centro storico)** 66,000
- **Inflation rate** 2.7%
- **Italian GDP per capita** US$22,100
- **Italian unemployment** 5.4%/ 11.5%/22% north/national/south

The mayor *(sindaco)*, Paolo Costa, has been in power at the head of a left-centre coalition since mid-2000 and is a stout defender of the controversial Mose project (see Environment p. 9).

ECONOMY

The mainstays of Venice's economy are tourism and the petrochemical industry concentrated in Porto Marghera on the mainland. The Veneto, long a rural backwater, has only taken off economically in recent decades, largely due to small industries and family businesses (such as Treviso-based Benetton). The Veneto contains 7.5% of Italy's population but contributes 12% of exports.

Tourism is pivotal in Venice. In 2000 the city's tourist board claimed 3.5 million visitors stayed at least one night in the lagoon city. As many as 15 million day-trippers (people who don't stay overnight and leave no statistical trace) pour in annually. The Veneto as a whole contributes 13% of all of Italy's tourist revenue.

Of the lagoon's remaining traditional industries, glass-making is the one with the most prominent profile. Although clearly directed at the tourist trade, some of the work coming out of Murano's glass factories remains of the highest quality.

Venice's once proud shipbuilding industry had already wilted to virtually nothing by the time the Venetian Republic fell in 1797.

SOCIETY & CULTURE

In 2000 the Venetian press got excited because the Veneto's population rose for the first time since 1983, by a staggering 1255 souls! As in the rest of country, the population is ageing and would be decreasing if it were not for immigration.

Once a country of emigrants, Italy is having trouble adjusting. Attitudes in Venice to the most visible immigrants, usually those having arrived illegally from Africa and Eastern Europe, tend not to be positive, although overt displays of racism remain fairly isolated.

Chiesa di Santa Maria della Visitazione

The majority of Venetians profess to be Catholics but many do not practise.

Venetians are generally a conservative and reserved lot. The standard form of greeting is the handshake. Kissing on both cheeks is only for people who know one another.

Dos and Don'ts

In churches you are expected to dress modestly. This means no shorts (for men or women) and no short skirts. Shoulders must be covered. These rules are enforced rigorously at St Mark's and some other churches. You have been warned!

ARTS

Venice is something of an outdoor museum and its galleries and churches are dripping with works from the city's glorious past. Modern art also gets a look in and occasionally temporary exhibitions amplify the range.

Although not a notable centre of contemporary art, the Biennale, Venice's biennial international visual arts fest, provides a chance to sample what's happening in art around the world.

Architecture

Apart from a few Roman vestiges found on Torcello and the mainland, the earliest reminders we have of building in the lagoon are the 7th and 9th century apses of the Cattedrale di Santa Maria Assunta on Torcello. The church is a mix of Byzantine and Romanesque. The latter style developed in the West and is characterised by simple construction and use of the semicircle for arches, windows, apses and so on. Byzantine influences are clearest in the use of mosaics in decoration but also in the way churches were arranged (including the iconostasis used in Eastern Orthodox churches).

By far the grandest example of style mixing is St Mark's Basilica (Basilica di San Marco). It is a grand Byzantine work, but with touches ranging from Romanesque to Renaissance.

Venice put its own spin on Gothic. Of the religious buildings, the two grand churches of the Franciscan and Dominican orders, the Frari and SS Giovanni e Paolo, are towering, austere creations in brick, largely rectilinear and eschewing much external decoration. The white and pink marble Doge's Palace (Palazzo Ducale) is the most stunning example of late-Gothic civil construction, while many houses that survive from the period can be identified by the clusters of windows that taper in an Oriental flourish at the top.

The Renaissance brought a return to the study of classical lines, never clearer than in Andrea Palladio's (1508-80) Chiesa di San Giorgio Maggiore and Chiesa del SS Redentore (Giudecca). Jacopo Sansovino (1486-1570) was another key Renaissance architect. The Baroque architect Baldassare Longhena (1598-1682) dominated the 17th century, just as his Chiesa di Santa Maria della Salute presides over the southern end of the Grand Canal.

Meander through the architectural styles of the maze-like outdoor museum of Venice.

Painting & Mosaic

A visit to St Mark's Basilica is sufficient to understand the importance of mosaic decor in Venetian art, largely influenced by the Byzantine Empire in the Middle Ages.

The first Venetian painter of note, Paolo Veneziano (c1300-62), wavered between the pre-Renaissance experimentation of the Florentine Giotto and a static Gothic style.

The glory days of Venetian art came with the Renaissance, starting with the Bellini family, especially Giovanni. He was followed by Vittore Carpaccio (1460-1526), Cima da Conegliano (c1459-c1517), Giorgione (1477-1510) and Lorenzo Lotto (c1480-1556). All have left works behind them in Venice. They laid the foundations for what was to come, a star-burst of greatness that thrust Venice into the forefront of European painting.

Detail of St Mark's dazzling mosaics

When his *Assunta* was unveiled in the Frari church, Titian (c1490-1576) was revealed as an unparalleled genius of the late Renaissance. He only just overshadowed Tintoretto (1518-94), best known for his paintings that fill the Scuola di San Rocco, and Paolo Veronese (1528-88), who had a hand in the decoration of the Doge's Palace and Libreria Nazionale Marciana. A lesser host of artists producing fine works beavered away in the shadow of these greats.

Things slipped in the 17th century until the arrival of Giambattista Tiepolo (1696-1770), the uncontested king of Venetian rococo, and his son Giandomenico (1727-1804). At about the same time another school of artists, the *vedutisti* (landscape painters), was also at work, led by Canaletto (1697-1768), whose photo-clear images of Venice are known the world over.

The neoclassicist Francesco Hayez (1791-1882) had a solid career, mostly in Milan, while Emilio Vedova (b1919) has dominated 20th century art in Venice. He began as an Expressionist but with time veered increasingly to the abstract.

Sculpture

Fine Romanesque sculpture adorns St Mark's Basilica, and some of the doges' tombs in the Chiesa di SS Giovanni e Paolo are worthy Gothic-era contributions. Overall, however, sculpture played second fiddle to painting in Venice.

Antonio Canova (1757-1822), born in Possagno, spent his early years in Venice but ended up in Rome as the country's most celebrated sculptor. A few of his works can be seen in the Museo Correr.

highlights

Millions of visitors stay only two or three days, but to even begin an acquaintance with Venice, weeks wouldn't suffice. Long-term residents never tire of the unexpected nooks and crannies they turn up in the course of wandering.

Although you have the option of the *vaporetto* (water bus), Venice is, more than most, a city for walkers. Water transport comes into its own for visiting other lagoon islands, some of which (such as Murano, Burano and Torcello) merit inclusion on your itinerary.

The crowds at St Mark's Basilica and the surrounding monuments can be overwhelming, but most of the city's remaining sights present few problems. Take time just to meander – losing yourself in the maze of canals and lanes is one of the principal pleasures Venice has to offer its visitors.

> ### Venice Lowlights
>
> Some things make you wish Venice would sink without trace:
>
> - Pigeons at St Mark's Square
> - Suffocating summer crowds in the main tourist spots
> - The cost and confusion of public transport
> - Rip-off restaurants and their touts

Confusing commuting

Stopping Over?

One Day Catch the No 1 vaporetto to St Mark's Square and visit St Mark's Basilica. Follow with a coffee at Caffè Florian and lunch in a nearby restaurant. Cross Ponte dell'Accademia for some serious art at the Gallerie dell'Accademia and Peggy Guggenheim Collection.

Two Days Sniff around the Rialto markets and shops in the San Polo district. Follow with high culture at the Frari and the Scuola Grande di San Rocco. Lose the afternoon wandering the Dorsoduro district and spend the evening eating and drinking around Campo Santa Margherita.

Three Days Explore the Doge's Palace, climb the Campanile, and take the ferry out to the islands of Murano, Burano and/or Torcello. Back in Venice, cede to the temptation of a gondola ride, a classy meal and a Bellini at Harry's Bar.

> ### Special Tickets
>
> A museum pass (€15.50, €10.35 students) covers admission to the Musei Civici (Civic Museums), ie Doge's Palace, Museo Correr, Museo Archeologico, Libreria Nazionale Marciana, Ca' Rezzonico, Museo Vetrario on Murano, Museo del Merletto on Burano, Palazzo Mocenigo and Casa di Goldoni. It is valid for three months.
>
> You can also buy a ticket (€9.30/ 5.20) for the Doge's Palace, Museo Correr, Museo Archeologico and Libreria Nazionale Marciana only. Further options include a €8.30/4.65 ticket for Ca' Rezzonico, Palazzo Mocenigo and the Casa di Goldoni, and a €6.20/4.15 ticket for the Murano and Burano museums.

BURANO (5, B9)

Famous for its lace industry, Burano is a pretty fishing village, its streets and canals lined with bright, pastel-coloured houses. The bon-bon colours apparently have their origins in the fishermen's desire to to see their own houses when heading home from a day at sea; and the gay colours are certainly engaging. Given the island's distance from Venice (around 40 minutes by ferry) you really do get the feeling of having arrived somewhere only fleetingly touched by La Serenissima.

The **Museo del Merletto** is Burano's lace-making museum. The islanders became famous for their lace in the late 19th century after the industry was resuscitated and lace-making schools were set up. If you plan to buy lace on the island, choose with care, as these days much of the cheaper stuff is factory produced. That said, you can still occasionally see women stitching away in the shade of their homes and in the parks.

INFORMATION

✉ Burano

🚇 Burano: No 12 from Fondamente Nuove

ⓘ Museo del Merletto, Piazza Galuppi 187 (☎ 041 73 00 34; Wed-Mon 10am-5pm; €4.15)

♿ limited

✗ Ristorante Galuppi (p. 88)

A Stitch in Time

Venetian lace was a much sought after commodity from the 15th century onwards but was eclipsed by French production in the 18th century. The industry was thankfully saved from extinction when lace schools were founded on the island of Burano, largely to alleviate poverty, at the end of the 19th century.

If you make the effort to visit (most people take in Murano and Torcello on the same trip), try to give yourself time to wander into the quietest corners and shady parks. Cross the wooden bridge to neighbouring **Mazzorbo** (which has its own vaporetto stop), a larger island with a few houses, a couple of trattorie and open green space. A snooze in the grass takes you light years from the marvels of Venice.

Strait-laced offerings on sale in Burano

DOGE'S PALACE (3, H14)

The Doge's Palace (Palazzo Ducale) is a rare example of civil Venetian Gothic and its predecessors. It was home to the *doge* (duke) and to all arms of government, including prisons, for much of the life of the Republic.

Established in the 9th century, the building began to assume its present form 500 years later, with the decision to build the massive Sala del Maggior Consiglio (Great Council or Parliament). The palace's two magnificent Gothic facades in white Istrian stone and pink Veronese marble face the water and Piazzetta San Marco. Much of the building was dam-

Damien Simons

aged by fire in 1577, but it was successfully restored by Antonio da Ponte (who also designed Ponte di Rialto).

The main courtyard is dominated at the northern end by the marble **Scala dei Giganti** (Giants' Staircase), topped by Sansovino's statues of Mars and Neptune.

Climb the stairs up to the 1st floor and follow the signs up Sansovino's grand **Scala d'Oro** (Golden Staircase). Just before you climb this staircase you pass a *bocca della verità* (mouth of truth) into which Venetians placed denunciations against whom they considered wayward citizens.

Halfway up the first flight of the Scala d'Oro, turn right and then up more stairs to reach the series of rooms comprising the Appart-

mento del Doge (Doge's Apartments). Among these, the grand **Sala delle Mappe** is interesting. It contains maps depicting the Republic's territories and the voyages of Marco Polo dating from 1762. You pass through several smaller rooms on the left wing before reaching the long hall known as the Sala dei Filosofi. Of particular interest is Titian's San Cristoforo (St Christopher), a fresco above a side stairwell (signposted). More rooms follow on the right wing. You follow these, cross the Sala delle Mappe again and turn upstairs to the next floor.

The highest organs of the government met in these rooms of the palace. You enter the **Sala delle Quattro Porte** (Four Doors Room; named for obvious reasons), where ambassadors would be requested to

DON'T MISS
• Museo dell'Opera • Veronese's paintings in the Sala del Consiglio dei Dieci • views from the 1st-floor galleries • Prigioni Nuove

await their ducal audience. Palladio designed the ceiling and Tintoretto added the frescoes.

Off this room is the **Anticollegio**, which features four Tintorettos and the *Ratto d'Europa* (Rape of Europa) by Veronese. Farther on is the splendid **Sala del Collegio**, the ceiling of which features a series of works by Veronese and a few by Tintoretto. Next is the **Sala del Senato**, graced by yet more Tintorettos. You progress through more rooms and the **Armeria** (Armoury) before being directed downstairs and to the immense **Sala del Maggiore Consiglio**. This is dominated at one end by Tintoretto's *Paradiso*, one of the world's largest oil paintings, measuring 22m by 7m. Among the many other paintings in the hall is a masterpiece, the *Apoteosi di Venezia* (Apotheosis of Venice) by Veronese, in one of the central ceiling panels.

From the northeastern end a trail of corridors leads you to the small, enclosed **Bridge of Sighs** (Ponte dei Sospiri). The bridge itself is split into two levels, allowing for traffic heading into and out of the **Prigioni Nuove** (New Prisons), built on the eastern side of the Rio di Palazzo della Paglia in the 16th century to cater for the overflow from the Prigioni Vecchie (Old Prisons) within the Doge's Palace itself.

Re-emerging from the prison, you re-cross the Bridge of Sighs and pass through further rooms and former offices before reaching the cafe and courtyard. Exit via what was traditionally the main entrance, Giovanni and Bartolomeo Bon's 15th century **Porta della Carta** (Paper Door), to which government decrees were fixed (hence the name).

Itinerari Segreti

The 'secret itineraries' is a 1½ hour guided tour (€12.40; book ahead on ☎ 041 522 49 51) of lesser-known areas of the palace, including the original Prigioni Vecchie (Old Prisons). Peak into the Inquisitor's Office and see how Casanova escaped from the Piombi (Leads), the sweltering roof prison cells.

Looking out to sea from the palace facade.

GALLERIE DELL'ACCADEMIA   (3, K6)

The Gallerie dell'Accademia form Venice's single most important art collection. The former church and convent of Santa Maria della Carità, with additions by Palladio, house a swathe of works that follows the progression of Venetian art from the 14th to the 18th centuries.

From the ticket office you pass upstairs to **Room (Sala) 1**, where the gallery's more or less chronological display begins. This hall, with its magnificent timber ceiling, is given over to religious art of the 14th century.

Room 2 contains paintings by Giovanni Bellini, Vittore Carpaccio and Cima da Conegliano. Note the commonality in themes adopted by all three in their depictions of the Madonna and child, for instance the musicians at the Madonna's feet. The most enthralling of the works is Carpaccio's altarpiece *Crocifissione e Apoteosi dei 10,000 Martiri del Monte Ararat* (Crucifixion and Apotheosis of the 10,000 Martyrs of Mt Ararat). More works by Giovanni Bellini and Cima da Conegliano adorn **Room 3**.

In **Rooms 4** and **5** you can enjoy a mixed bag, including some non-Venetians. They include Andrea Mantegna's *San Giorgio* (St George) and works by Cosmè Tura, Piero della Francesca and Jacopo Bellini. Observe in Bellini's pieces the comparative stiffness of the characters, a faithful reflection of a style still crossing over from Gothic.

His son Giovanni has 11 paintings here and the greater suppleness of expression is clear – take the remarkable *Madonna col Bambino tra le Sante Caterina e Maddalena* (Madonna with Child Between Sts Catherine and Mary Magdalen) as an example.

The most striking paintings in these rooms are the two rare contributions by Giorgione: *La Tempesta* (The Storm) and *La Vecchia* (The Old Woman). Look at the latter closely. The lines and brush strokes, the look in the eyes, indeed the very subject matter, belong to another century. Its complete lack of stylisation makes it readily identifiable with 19th century portraiture.

In **Room 6** are six works each by Tintoretto and Veronese and one by Titian. In Tintoretto's *La Creazione degli Animali* (The Creation of the Animals) we can see the thick splashy paint-strokes that characterised much of this Mannerist's work.

The main interest in **Rooms 7** and **8** is Lorenzo Lotto's *Ritratto del Giovane Gentiluomo nel Suo Studio* (Portrait of a Young Gentleman in His

Studio). What's the lizard doing on his desk? Others represented here are Titian, Palma il Vecchio and even Giorgio Vasari.

In **Room 10** we are confronted by some major works, one of the highlights of which is Paolo Veronese's *Convito in Casa di Levi* (Feast in the House of Levi). The room also contains one of Titian's last works, *Pietà*. The nightmarish quality of the faces has a Goyaesque touch. Finally, there are some remarkable Tintorettos dedicated to the theme of St Mark. Another fine Tintoretto is his *Crocifissione* (Crucifixion) in **Room 11**.

Cry Freedom

Paolo Veronese's version of the *Ultima Cena* (Last Supper) for the Chiesa dei SS Giovanni e Paolo got him into hot water with the Inquisition, which found figures in the painting, such as a jester and dog, impious. Veronese's spirited defence of artistic freedom of expression did not cut the mustard and he was ordered to eliminate all offending images. The leaders of La Serenissima, no friends of the Holy Office, backed a compromise and made Veronese rename his work *Convito in Casa di Levi* (Feast in the House of Levi) instead.

Rooms 12 to **19** are of lesser interest but just as you think the exhibition is losing steam, you enter **Room 20**. The crowd scenes, splashes of red and activity pouring from the canvases in this cycle dedicated to the *Miracoli della Vera Croce* (Miracles of the True Cross) are a vivid record of Venetian life. They were carried out by Carpaccio, Gentile Bellini and others for the Scuola Grande di San Giovanni Evangelista (p. 42), home to a relic of the True Cross.

Carpaccio's extraordinary series of nine paintings recounting the life of Santa Orsola, in **Room 21**, is the collection's last high point.

APL/Corbis

Left: Admire the views from the Ponte dell'Accademia before crossing to the Gallerie.
Above: Courtyard of Gallerie dell'Accademia, once a church and convent

DON'T MISS
• Tintoretto's *Assunzione della Vergine* and *Trafugamento del Corpo di San Marco* • Tiepolo's *Castigo dei Serpenti* • art in the former Santa Maria della Carità • Titian's *Presentazione di Maria al Tempio*

GHETTO (4, B5)

The first records of Jews in Venice (Ashkenazi of German and Eastern European origins) date back to the 10th century. In 1382 the Maggior Consiglio (Venetian Parliament) decreed that Jews were allowed to operate as moneylenders.

Damien Simons

INFORMATION

- ✉ Ghetto
- e www.ghetto.it
- 🚢 Guglie: Nos 41, 42, 51 & 52
- ⓘ Museo Ebraico, Campo di Ghetto Nuovo, Cannaregio 2902/b (☎ 041 71 53 59; Sun-Fri 10am-7pm, except Jewish holidays; €2.60); guided tours of the Ghetto: €6.20 inc museum; Sun-Fri hourly 10.30am-5.30pm, except Jewish holidays
- ♿ limited
- ✗ Gam Gam (p. 84)

Snow clad gateway to the Ghetto

In 1516 all Jews were ordered to live in one area. The Getto Novo (New Foundry) was considered ideal, being surrounded by water – a natural prison. The Ashkenazis' harsh Germanic pronunciation gave us the word ghetto.

Jews could move freely through the city if they wore a yellow cap or badge. At midnight gates around the Ghetto Nuovo were shut by Christian guards financed by the Jewish community, and reopened at dawn.

Excluded from most professions, Jews had few career options. Most got along as moneylenders or in the rag trade. Two 'banks' (benches) from which moneylenders operated remain in evidence on Campo di Ghetto Nuovo, Banco Rosso and Banco Verde. A third career option was medicine. Jews from Spain or the Middle East had benefited from the advances in the Arab world and were considered better doctors than their Christian counterparts.

A quick look around will reveal how small the Ghetto was. Overcrowding turned the buildings around Campo di Ghetto Nuovo into Venice's 'skyscrapers' – some apartment blocks have seven storeys, with very low ceilings. Atop three were built modest *schole* (synagogues). The **Schola Tedesca** (German Synagogue) is above the building that now houses the Museo Ebraico (p. 21). Virtually next door is the **Schola Canton** (Corner Synagogue) and farther around is the **Schola Italiana**, the simplest of the three.

In 1541 waves of Levantine Jews from Spain and Portugal arrived, many of them wealthy merchants, and the town authorities ceded another small area to the Jews, the Getto Vecio (Old Foundry). This came to be known as the Old Ghetto, although the converse was true (the foundry was old but the Jewish community was new). Here the Spanish and Portuguese built their two synagogues, the **Schola Spagnola** (at the southern end of Campiello della Schole) and the **Schola Levantina**. They are considered the most beautiful in northern Italy.

A final small territorial concession was wrung from the town authorities when a street south of the Ghetto Nuovo, subsequently known as the Calle del Ghetto Nuovissimo (Very New Ghetto St), was granted to the Jews.

From 1541 until 1553 the Jewish community thrived. Their money and trade were welcome and the community built a reputation for book printing. Then Pope Julian banned such activities and things went downhill.

In 1797 Napoleon abolished all restrictions on Jews and in 1866 all minorities were guaranteed full equality before the law.

In 1943, many of Venice's 1670 Jews were interned under race laws and some 200 wound up in a Polish death camp. Altogether, about 8000 Italian Jews were killed in the Holocaust. About 30 Jews live in the Ghetto today.

The **Museo Ebraico** (Jewish Museum) contains a modest collection of Jewish religious silverware. The guided tours (in Italian or English; other languages if booked in advance) of the Ghetto and three of its synagogues (Schola Canton, Schola Italiana and Schola Levantina) that leave from the museum are highly recommended. The interior of the Schola Levantina betrays a hefty rococo influence, best seen in the decor of the pulpit. The Schola Levantina is used for Saturday prayers in winter (it has heating) while the Schola Spagnola (which can't be visited) is used in summer.

Tough Rulebook

Historically, Jews in Venice had many rules to observe. Until they were assigned the Ghetto, they had long been forbidden to reside steadily in the city of Venice and could not stay there for more than 15 days at a time (most lived in Mestre and Giudecca). They were not allowed to buy houses or have relations with Christian women.

Minority markings

CA' D'ORO (3, A10)

This magnificent Gothic structure built in the 15th century got its name (Golden House) from the gilding that originally decorated the sculptural details of the facade. Visible from the Grand Canal, the facade stands out remarkably from the remainder of the edifice, which is rather drab by comparison.

INFORMATION

- ✉ Calle di Ca' d'Oro, Cannaregio 3931
- ☎ 041 523 87 90
- 🚤 Ca' d'Oro: Nos 1, 82 & N
- ⏱ Tues-Sun 8.15am-7.15pm, Mon 8.15am-2pm
- 💲 €3.10
- ♿ limited
- 🍴 Osteria dalla Vedova (p. 85)

Damien Simonis

Get up close to the Ca' d'Oro's facade.

Damien Simonis

Ca' d'Oro houses the **Galleria Franchetti**, an impressive collection consisting of bronzes, tapestries and paintings. The 1st floor is devoted mainly to religious painting, sculpture and bronzes from the 15th and early 16th centuries. One of the first items you come across is a polyptych recounting the martyrdom of St Bartholomew (San Bartolomeo). Take a closer look at the detail. The violence is quite remarkable, as is the saintly indifference with which Bartholomew seems to accept his torment! Much of what you see on this floor is Venetian, but one room has been set aside principally for Tuscan art.

On the 2nd floor you can see a series of fragments of frescoes saved from the outside of the Fondaco dei Tedeschi (p. 40), an important trading house that is now home to the central post office. All but one are by Titian.

The other, a nude by Giorgione, is the most striking, however. Also on this floor is a mixed collection, including works by Tintoretto, Carpaccio, Mantegna, Vivarini, Titian, Signorelli and van Eyck.

A big incentive for visiting is the chance to lean out from the balconies over the Grand Canal on the 1st and 2nd floors. Staff will start hustling you out half an hour before actual closing time.

The Star & his Master

Titian has been called the 'sun amidst the stars'. But he started under the direction of Giorgione and experts have difficulty distinguishing some of their works. They first collaborated on the Fondaco dei Tedeschi frescoes. Even after Giorgione's death in 1510, Titian continued to work under the spell of his former master.

GRAND CANAL (3 & 4)

This is Main St Venice, a broad ribbon of colours, sounds and smells in the shape of an inverted 'S'. Jump on the No 1 all-stops vaporetto at Piazzale Roma (3, D1) or Ferrovia (3, B2) for the half-hour meander along the world's most extraordinary traffic artery.

The 3.5km canal, probably once a natural extension of the River Brenta before the latter was diverted, supports an ever changing parade of transport barges, vaporetti, water taxis, private speedboats, gondolas, police patrol boats, water ambulances and water fire brigade. The floating pageant is backed on either side by more than 100 *palazzi* (mansions) dating from the 12th to the 18th centuries.

Just after the Riva de Biasio stop (4, E5) is the **Fondaco dei Turchi** (p. 54), recognisable by the three-storey towers on either side of its colonnade.

INFORMATION

✉ Grand Canal
🚢 Nos 1, 3, 4, 82 & N
♿ good

Past Rio di San Marcuola, the **Palazzo Vendramin-Calergi** (p. 41) is on the left. To the right, just after the San Stae stop (3, A8), you'll see the **Ca' Pesaro**, which houses the Galleria d'Arte Moderna and Museo d'Arte Orientale (p. 38). Shortly after, to the left, is the **Ca' d'Oro** (p. 22), beyond which the boat turns towards the 16th century **Ponte di Rialto** (p. 49) and the **Rialto produce markets** (p. 76).

The vaporetto sweeps on past more fine mansions to the wooden **Ponte dell'Accademia** (p. 49), where you get off for the art gallery of the same name (p. 18), and on past the grand **Chiesa di Santa Maria della Salute** (p. 32) before reaching San Marco.

No real traffic jams, but there's still a riot of colour and noise on the Grand Canal.

DON'T MISS
• Ca' Foscari (3, G5) • Palazzo Grassi (3, G6) • Palazzo Dario's marble facade (3, K9) • Palazzo Corner (3, J8)

LIDO DI VENEZIA (5, 8E)

On summer weekends Venetians flock here to the beach, but the high rollers who used to accompany them go elsewhere now that the former summer casino is closed. In September celebs from all over crowd into the **Palazzo della Mostra del Cinema** for the Venice film festival (p. 93).

INFORMATION

- ✉ Lido di Venezia
- 🚊 Lido: Nos 1, 6, 14, 20, 51, 52, 61, 62, 82 & N
- ⓘ Antico Cimitero Israelitico, Riviera San Nicolò (☎ 041 71 53 59; €6.20); guided visits (in Italian & English) Fri 10.30am, Wed & Sun 2.30pm
- ♿ good

Dallas Stribley

Dallas Stribley

All change! Bathing huts on a Lido beach

The Lido forms a long, narrow land barrier between the lagoon and the Adriatic. For centuries, the doges sailed out to fulfil Venice's Marriage to the Sea ceremony by dropping a ring into the shallows, celebrating the close relationship between city and sea. This was done just off the **Chiesa di San Nicolò**, at the northern end of the island.

A few hundred metres south of the church is the **Antico Cimitero Israelitico** (Former Jewish Cemetery). You can turn up at the gates or buy tickets at the Museo Ebraico (p. 21) in Cannaregio to tour the burial ground, the second oldest Jewish cemetery in Europe after that in Worms (Germany).

The Lido became a fashionable seaside resort in the 19th century and most of the beaches along the northern half of the island charge an arm and a leg.

Bus B or a rental bicycle will take you about 10km from the vaporetto stop to **Malamocco**, in the south. It is arranged across a chain of squares and canals and is more reminiscent of Venice than the turn-of-the-century seaside conceits farther north. Also at the southern end of the island are the pleasant (and free) beaches of **Alberoni**.

Death in Venice

It is on the fashionable but melancholy beaches of the Lido that the wan figure of Aschenbach, portrayed by Dirk Bogarde in the film version of Thomas Mann's novel *Der Tod in Venedig* (Death in Venice), slumps on a beach chair as he obsesses about a young boy. Some things haven't changed and Italians still use the little cabins to change into their swimming costumes and store their bits and bobs.

MURANO (5, C7)

The people of Venice have been making crystal and glass (the difference between the two lies in the amount of lead used) since as early as the 10th century, when the secrets of the art were brought back from the East by merchants. The bulk of the industry was moved to the island of Murano in 1291 because of the danger of fire posed by the glass-working furnaces.

Venice had a virtual monopoly on the production of what is now known as Murano glass and the methods of the craft were such a well guarded secret that it was considered treason for a glass-worker to leave the city.

The incredibly elaborate pieces can range from the beautiful to the grotesque. Watching the glass-workers in action in factories on the island is certainly interesting. You can see them in several outlets along Fondamenta dei Vetrai and a couple on Viale Garibaldi. Look for the sign 'Fornace' (furnace). The **Museo Vetrario** has some exquisite pieces.

The nearby **Chiesa dei SS Maria e Donato** is a fascinating example of Veneto-Byzantine architecture, mixed in with Romanesque (see the apse). It was rededicated to San Donato after his bones were brought here from Cephalonia, along with those of a dragon he had supposedly killed (four of the 'dragon' bones are hung behind the altar). The church's magnificent mosaic pavement was laid in the 12th century, and the impressive mosaic of the Virgin Mary in the apse dates from the same period.

Contemporary twist on a traditional trade

INFORMATION

- ✉ Murano
- 🚏 Colonna or Faro: Nos 12, 13, 41, 42, 71 & 72
- ① Museo Vetrario, Fondamenta Giustinian 8 (☎ 041 73 95 86; Tues-Thurs 10am-5pm; €5.20)
- ♿ limited
- ✗ Osteria dalla Mora (p. 88)

DON'T MISS
- occasional glass exhibitions in Palazzo da Mula • Palazzo Trevisan
- colourful Canale di San Donato

MUSEO CORRER   (3, H12)

The Ala Napoleonica (Napoleonic Wing) that closes off the western end of St Mark's Square is now home to the Museo Correr, dedicated to the art and history of Venice.

Once inside, you turn right into a hall lined with statuary and bas-reliefs by Canova. More of his creations adorn the following couple of rooms, which are collectively known as the **Sale Neoclassiche** (Neoclassical Rooms). Keeping the statues company is an assortment of 19th-century paintings, books, documents, medallions, musical instruments and other bits.

Next come the rooms dedicated to **Civiltà Veneziana** (Venetian Civilisation), where you can inspect coins and standards of the Republic, model galleys, maps, navigation instruments and a display of weaponry from bygone days.

You are encouraged to continue straight on to the **Museo Archeologico**, crammed mostly with Greek and Roman statues, along with a vast collection of ancient coins and ceramics. Some of the material, but by no means all, was collected in the Veneto.

Afterwards comes the **Libreria Nazionale Marciana**. The Sala della Libreria is the main reading hall and was built in the 16th century to house the collection of some 1000 codices left to the Republic by Cardinal Bessarione in 1468. The ceiling was decorated by a battalion of artists chosen by Titian and Sansovino, the architect. Of them, Veronese was considered the best; his three contributions form the second line of medallions after you enter.

You then pass into the Vestibolo (Vestibule). The centrepiece of the ceiling ornamentation is Titian's *Sapienza* (Wisdom).

INFORMATION

- ✉ Piazza San Marco, San Marco 52
- ☎ 041 522 56 25
- e www.comune
  .venezia.it/museicivici
- 🚤 Vallaresso, San Marco & San Zaccaria: Nos 1, 3, 4, 6, 14, 41, 42, 51, 52, 71, 72, 82 & N
- ⏰ Apr-Oct: 9am-7pm; Nov-Mar: 9am-5pm
- 💲 €9.30
- ⓘ free guided tours of Museo Archeologico (in English): Mon-Fri 3pm; Sat-Sun noon, 3pm & 5pm; free guided tours of the library (in Italian & English): Sat-Sun 10am, noon, 2pm & 4pm
- ♿ limited
- 🍴 museum cafe

Venice's home for its cultural heritage

Christopher Groenhout

Damien Simonis

DON'T MISS   • Arte Antica collection • miniature bronzes

PEGGY GUGGENHEIM COLLECTION (3, K8)

The eccentric millionaire art collector Peggy Guggenheim called the unfinished **Palazzo Venier dei Leoni** home for 30 years, until she died in 1979. She left behind a collection of works by her favourite modern artists, representing most of the major movements of the 20th century.

The Palazzo Venier dei Leoni was so called because, it is said, the Venier family kept lions here! Peggy preferred dogs – many of them are buried alongside her grave in the sculpture garden.

Most of the collection is in the **east wing**. Early Cubist paintings include Picasso's *The Poet* (1911) and *Pipe, Glass, Bottle of Vieux Marc* (1914), and Georges Braque's *The Clarinet* (1912). The list of greats of 20th century art is long. There are a couple of Kandinskys, including his *Upward* (1929). Interesting works from Spain include Dalí's *Birth of Liquid Desires* (1932) and Miró's *Seated Woman II* (1939).

Among the many paintings of Max Ernst, Guggenheim's husband and doyen of Surrealism, is the disturbing *The Antipope* (1942). Other names to look for include: Jackson Pollock, Mark Rothko, Willem de Kooning, Paul Delvaux, Alexander Calder, Juan Gris, Kurt Schwitters, Paul Klee,

Damien Simonis

Damien Simonis

The glorious Guggenheim garden

Francis Bacon, Giorgio de Chirico, Piet Mondrian and Marc Chagall. Out in the **sculpture garden** are several pieces by Henry Moore and Jean Arp.

The **rear** of the mansion hosts a separate collection of Italian Futurists and other modern artists from the peninsula, including Giorgio Morandi, Giacomo Balla and one work by Amedeo Modigliani.

Peggy's Peregrinations

Miss Guggenheim came into her fortune in 1921 and set off for Europe where she became interested in contemporary art and opened a gallery (Guggenheim Jeune in London). As the Nazis bore down on Paris in 1940, Peggy was there looking for acquisitions. She spent the war in New York and moved to Venice in 1947.

ST MARK'S BASILICA (3, G13)

St Mark's Basilica (Basilica di San Marco), consecrated in 1094, embodies a magnificent blend of architectural and decorative styles, dominated by the Byzantine and ranging from Romanesque and Gothic to Renaissance.

INFORMATION

- ✉ Piazza San Marco, San Marco
- ☎ 041 522 56 97
- 🚤 Vallaresso, San Marco & San Zaccaria: Nos 1, 3, 4, 6, 14, 41, 42, 51, 52, 71, 72, 82 & N
- ⏰ Mon-Sat 9.30am-5pm, Sun & hols 2-5pm
- 💲 Pala d'Oro €1.55; Tesoro €2.10; Galleria €1.55
- ♿ limited

Damien Simons

It was built on a Greek cross plan, with five bulbous domes, and modelled on Constantinople's Church of the Twelve Apostles (later destroyed). It was built as the doges' private chapel and only became **Venice's cathedral** in 1807.

For more than 500 years, the doges enlarged and embellished the church, adorning it with an incredible array of treasures plundered from the East.

The arches above the doorways in the **facade** boast fine mosaics. The one at the left end, depicting the arrival of St Mark's body in Venice, was completed in 1270. Above the doorway next to it is an 18th century mosaic depicting the doge venerating St Mark's body. The mosaics on the other side of the main doorway both date from the 17th century.

The only original **entrance** is the one on the southern side that leads to the **battistero** (baptistry). It is fronted by two pillars brought to Venice from Acre in the Holy Land in the 13th century. The 4th century Syriac sculpture, *Tetrarchi* (Tetrarchs), next to the Porta della Carta of the Doge's Palace, is believed to represent Diocletian and his three co-emperors, who ruled the Roman Empire in the 3rd century AD.

On the **Loggia dei Cavalli** above the main door are copies of four gilded bronze horses; the originals, on display inside, were stolen when Constantinople was sacked in 1204, during the Fourth Crusade.

Stolen saint: St Mark (represented by the winged lion) stands proudly in the basilica.

Damien Simonis

Through the doors is the **narthex**, or vestibule, its domes and arches decorated with mosaics, mainly dating from the 13th century. The oldest mosaics in the basilica, dating from 1063, are in the niches of the bay in front of the main door from the narthex into the church. They feature the Madonna with the apostles.

The **interior** of the basilica is dazzling; if you can take your eyes off the glitter of the mosaics, take time to admire the 12th century marble pavement, an infinite variety of geometrical whimsy interspersed with floral motifs and depictions of animals. The lower level of the walls is lined with precious Eastern marbles, and above this decoration the feast of gilded **mosaics** begins. Work started on them in the 11th century and continued until well into the 13th century and beyond.

Dress Code

A strict dress code operates at St Mark's. You will not be allowed in with shorts on (unless they cover the knees) and women must cover their shoulders and upper arms. People are turned away every day, often after queuing for hours, for not respecting this rule.

Separating the main body of the church from the high altar is a multicoloured marble **iconostasis**, divided in two by a huge cross of bronze and silver. Lining up on each side are the Virgin Mary and the apostles. Beneath the majestic marble **altar maggiore** (high altar) lie the remains of St Mark.

Behind the altar is the exquisite **Pala d'Oro**, a gold, enamel and jewel encrusted altarpiece made in Constantinople for Doge Pietro Orseolo I in 976. It was enriched and reworked in Constantinople in 1105, enlarged by Venetian

Full of Eastern promise

goldsmiths in 1209 and again reset in the 14th century. Among the almost 2000 precious stones that adorn it are emeralds, rubies, amethysts, sapphires and pearls.

The **Tesoro** (Treasury), accessible from the right transept, contains most of the booty from the 1204 raid on Constantinople, including a thorn said to be from the crown worn by Christ.

Through a door at the far right end of the narthex is a stairway leading up to the **Galleria** (aka Museo di San Marco), which contains the original gilded bronze horses and the **Loggia dei Cavalli**.

DON'T MISS
• carvings on the main doorway • the basilica illuminated
• Ascension mosaic • mosaics between the windows of the apse

ST MARK'S SQUARE (3, G13)

By day, hordes of tourists and pigeons flock to Venice's grandest square. Late at night it is eerily still. Either way, lined by the arcades of the **Procuratie Vecchie** and **Procuratie Nuove** (once the offices of the Procurators of St Mark), it appears as a spectacular theatre set.

At its eastern end rises the voluptuous facade of **St Mark's Basilica** (p. 28), the gorgeous religious heart of La Serenissima. Towering aloof above all comers is the **Campanile**, the church's sturdy brick bell tower. Stand and wait for the bronze Mori (Moors) to strike the bell of the 15th century **Torre dell'Orologio**, which rises above the entrance to the **Mercerie**, the series of streets that forms the main thoroughfare north from San Marco to the Rialto.

Among the arcades of the Procuratie you can sit and savour an expensive coffee at Florian, Quadri or Lavena, the 18th century cafes facing each other on the piazza. The piazza is closed off to the west by another arcade, the **Ala Napoleonica**. Now home to the Museo Correr, it was built by Napoleon in memory of his own greatness.

South of the square is the contiguous **Piazzetta San Marco**, lined by the Doge's Palace and Sansovino's **Libreria Nazionale Marciana**. At the water's edge Venice's two patron saints, St Mark (represented by the lion) and St Theodore, seemingly guard the sea entrance to the heart of Venice. Many an unfortunate has been executed between them over the centuries.

Not everyone thinks the pigeons are pesky!

DON'T MISS
- Campanile views (p. 40) • shopping in the nearby fashionable Frezzeria (3, G11)

SAN GIORGIO MAGGIORE (2, H10)

On the island of the same name, Palladio's Chiesa di San Giorgio Maggiore has one of the most prominent positions in Venice and, although it inspired mixed reactions among the architect's contemporaries, it had a significant influence on Renaissance architecture.

Built between 1565 and 1580, it is possibly Palladio's most imposing structure in Venice. The **facade**, although not erected until the following century, is believed to conform with Palladio's wishes. The massive columns on high plinths, crowning tympanum and statues contain an element of sculptural chiaroscuro, casting strong shadows and reinforcing the impression of strength. Facing the Bacino di San Marco and the heart of Venice, its effect is deliberately theatrical.

Damien Simons

Inside, the sculptural decoration is sparse, the open space regimented by powerful clusters of columns and covered by luminous vaults.

An Ignoble Fate

The great Benedictine convent of San Giorgio Maggiore was suppressed after the fall of the Venetian Republic in 1797. The island was turned into a free port and the Austrians set up an artillery base here. By the end of WWII, the island had fallen into decay and was largely saved by the Fondazione Cini.

San Giorgio Maggiore's **art treasures** include Tintoretto's *Ultima Cena* (Last Supper) and the *Raccolta della Manna* (Shower of Manna) on the walls of the high altar, and a *Deposizione* (Deposition) in the Cappella dei Morti. Take the lift to the top of the 60m-high **bell tower** for an extraordinary view.

Behind the church extend the **grounds of the former monastery**. Established in the 10th century by the Benedictines, it was rebuilt in the 13th century and then restructured and expanded in a series of projects that spanned the 16th century, finishing with the library built by Longhena in the 1640s. Little of this can be seen, as the **Fondazione Cini**, a cultural foundation, bought it in 1951.

Damien Simons

San Giorgio Maggiore's striking facade

SANTA MARIA DELLA SALUTE (3, K10)

Baldassare Longhena's dazzling white monolith is possibly the city's most familiar silhouette (viewed from Piazzetta San Marco or the Ponte dell'Accademia), but seen from close up it's difficult to take in.

INFORMATION

- ✉ Campo della Salute, Dorsoduro 1/b
- ☎ 041 522 55 58
- 🚤 Salute: No 1
- 🕐 9am-noon, 3-5.30pm
- ⑤ sacristy €1.05
- ♿ limited
- ✗ Ai Gondolieri (p. 81)

Damien Simonis

A crown for the mother of God

Longhena got the commission to build the church in honour of the Virgin Mary, who was believed to have delivered the city from an outbreak of plague in 1630. The ranks of statues that festoon the **exterior** of the church culminate in one of the Virgin Mary atop the dome.

The octagonal form of the church is unusual. Longhena's idea was to design it in the form of a crown for the mother of God. The **interior** is flooded with light pouring through windows in the walls and dome. Dominating the main body of the church is the extraordinary Baroque **altar maggiore** (high altar), in which is imbedded an icon of Mary brought to Venice from Crete.

The **sacristy** ceiling is bedecked with three remarkable Titians. The figures depicted are so full of curvaceous movement they almost seem to be caught in a washing machine! The three scenes are replete with high emotion, depicting the struggles between

Caino e Abele (Cain and Abel), *David e Golia* (David and Goliath) and finally between Abraham and his conscience in *Il Sacrificio di Isaaco* (The Sacrifice of Isaac). The other star of the sacristy is Tintoretto's *Le Nozze di Cana* (The Wedding Feast of Cana), filled with an unusual amount of bright and cheerful light by Tintoretto's rather dark standards.

Walking on Water

Every year, on 21 November, a procession takes place from St Mark's Square to the Santa Maria della Salute to give thanks for the city's good health. The last part of the march takes place on a pontoon bridge thrown out between the Santa Maria del Giglio *traghetto* stop and the church.

SANTA MARIA GLORIOSA DEI FRARI (3, E5)

Built for the Franciscans in the 14th and 15th centuries of brick and on a Latin cross plan (with three naves and a transept), this spare Gothic church impresses with its high vaulted ceiling and by its sheer size. A visit inside the church is a must on any art lover's tour of the city.

The simplicity of the **interior** (red and white marble floor, with the same colours dominating the walls and ceiling) is more than offset by the extravagance of decoration in the form of paintings and funereal monuments. Also, the middle of the central nave is filled by the choir stalls, an unusual appearance in Italian churches (although common in Spain).

The mastery of **Titian** is, however, the main attraction of the Frari. His dramatic *Assunta* (Assumption; 1518) over the high altar represents a key moment in his rise as one of the city's greatest artists, praised unreservedly by all and sundry as a work of inspired genius.

Another of his masterpieces, the *Madonna di Ca' Pesaro* (Madonna of Ca' Pesaro), hangs above the Pesaro altar (in the left hand aisle, near the choir stalls). Also of note are: Giovanni Bellini's triptych, in the apse of the sacristy; Donatello's statue *Giovanni Battista* (John the Baptist), in the first chapel to the right of the high altar; and Vivarini's *Sant' Ambrogio in Trono e Santi* (St Ambrose Enthroned and Saints), in the second-last chapel to the left of the high altar.

INFORMATION

✉ Campo dei Frari, San Polo 3004
☎ 041 522 26 37
🚏 San Tomà: Nos 1, 82 & N
🕐 Mon-Sat 9am-6pm, Sun 1-6pm
💲 €1.55
♿ limited
✗ Arca (p. 81)

The giant Frari: a Titian treasure trove

A Chorus Line

An organisation called Chorus offers visitors a special three day ticket (€7.75) providing entry to all the churches where an admission price is charged. Those covered are: Santa Maria Gloriosa dei Frari, Santa Maria del Giglio (detail pictured top left), Santo Stefano, Santa Maria Formosa, Santa Maria dei Miracoli, San Polo, San Stae, Sant'Alvise, La Madonna dell'Orto, San Pietro di Castello, San Giacomo dell'Orio, SS Redentore and San Sebastiano. Admission to each will otherwise cost you €1.55. The ticket, which is available from any of the churches, includes the option to visit the Treasury (Tesoro) of St Mark's Basilica. See ⒺⒺ www.provincia.venezia.it/chorus for more details.

SCUOLA GRANDE DI SAN ROCCO   (3, E4)

Antonio Scarpagnino's (c1505-49) Renaissance **facade** (exhibiting a hint of the Baroque to come), with its white-marble columns and overbearing magnificence, seems uncomfortably squeezed into the tight space of the narrow square below it. Whatever you make of the exterior of this religious confraternity, or scuola, dedicated to St Roch, nothing can prepare you for what lies inside.

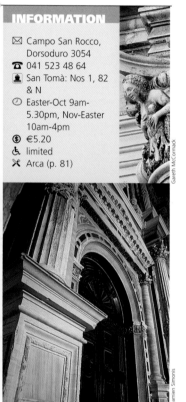

INFORMATION

✉ Campo San Rocco,
   Dorsoduro 3054
☎ 041 523 48 64
🚊 San Tomà: Nos 1, 82
   & N
🕐 Easter-Oct 9am-
   5.30pm, Nov-Easter
   10am-4pm
⑤ €5.20
♿ limited
✕ Arca (p. 81)

Gareth McCormack

Damien Simons

San Rocco's Renaissance grandeur

Plague Prevention

St Roch was born in Montpellier (France) in 1295, and at the age of 20 began wandering through Italy and southern France helping victims of the plague whom he encountered. He died in 1327 and a cult soon grew around his name. His body was transferred to Venice as a kind of plague prevention measure in 1485.

After winning a competition (Veronese was among his rivals), **Tintoretto** went on to devote 23 years of his life to decorating the school. The overwhelming concentration of more than 50 paintings by the master is altogether too much for the average human to digest.

Chronologically speaking, you should start upstairs (Scarpagnino designed the staircase) in the **Sala Grande Superiore**. Here you can pick up mirrors to carry around to avoid getting a sore neck while inspecting the ceiling paintings (which depict Old Testament episodes). Around the walls are scenes from the New Testament. A handful of works by other artists (such as Titian, Giorgione and Tiepolo) can also be seen. To give your eyes a rest from the paintings, inspect the woodwork below them – it is studded with curious designs, including a false book collection.

Downstairs, the walls of the confraternity's **assembly hall** feature a series on the life of the Virgin Mary, starting on the left wall with the *Annunciazione* and ending with the *Assunzione* opposite.

SS GIOVANNI E PAOLO (3, C15)

This huge Gothic church, founded by the Dominicans and completed in 1430, rivals the Franciscans' Frari (p. 33) in size and grandeur. The similarities between the two, such as the use of brick and the red and white chequerboard floor inside, are evident.

The **interior** is divided into an enormous central nave and two aisles, separated by graceful, soaring arches. A **stained-glass window** made in Murano in the 15th century (restored in the 1980s) fills the southern arm of the transept with light. A host of artists contributed to the window's design, including Bartolomeo Vivarini, Cima da Conegliano and Girolamo Mocetto. Below the window and just to the right is a fine **pala** (altarpiece) by Lorenzo Lotto. On the opposite aisle wall, below the organ, is a triptych by Bartolomeo Vivarini. Noteworthy, too, are the five late-Gothic **apses**, graced by long and slender windows. Look out for Giovanni Bellini's polyptych of St Vincent Ferrer (San Vincenzo Ferreri) over the second

Damien Simons

INFORMATION

- ✉ Campo SS Giovanni e Paolo, Castello 6363
- ☎ 041 523 75 10
- 🚤 Ospedale Civile: Nos 41, 42, 51 & 52
- ⏲ Mon-Sat 7.30am-12.30pm & 3.30-7pm, Sun 3-6pm
- 💲 free
- ♿ limited
- ✗ Ostaria al Ponte (p. 85)

Damien Simons

Gothic SS Giovanni e Paolo

Bragadin Bites the Dust

When the Turks took Famagusta (Cyprus) in 1570, they reserved a special fate for the Venetian commander, Marcantonio Bragadin. Having lopped off his nose and ears and left him to rot for a couple of weeks in a dungeon, he was then tortured and skinned alive. According to one account he only passed out when they reached his waist. The corpse was beheaded and the skin was stuffed with straw and sent to Constantinople. His remains, stolen in 1596, lie in the Chiesa dei SS Giovanni e Paolo.

altar of the right aisle.

In the **Cappella del Rosario**, off the northern arm of the transept, is a series of paintings by Paolo Veronese, including ceiling panels and an *Adorazione dei Pastori* (Adoration of the Shepherds).

The church is a ducal pantheon. Around the walls, many of the 25 **tombs** of doges were sculpted by prominent Gothic and Renaissance artists, in particular Pietro and Tullio Lombardo.

TORCELLO (5, A9)

This delightful island, with its overgrown main square and sparse, scruffy-looking buildings and monuments, was at its peak from the mid-7th century to the 13th century, when it was the seat of the bishop of mainland Altinum (modern Altino) and home to 20,000 souls. Today, fewer than 80 people remain.

Damien Simons

Take in the views from Torcello's tower.

A 10 minute walk from the vaporetto stop lies the square around which huddles all that remains of old Torcello – the lasting homes of the clergy and the island's secular rulers.

The **Cattedrale di Santa Maria Assunta** was founded in the 7th century and was Venice's first – in the early days this was the leading lagoon settlement. What you see of the church today dates from its first expansion in 824 and rebuilding in 1008. It is therefore about the oldest Venetian monument to have remained relatively untampered with.

The three apses (the central one dates from the original structure) have a Romanesque quality. The magnificent **Byzantine mosaics** inside, dating from the 12th and 13th centuries, are fascinating. On the western wall is a vast mosaic depicting the Last Judgment. Hell (lower right side) does not look any fun at all. The greatest treasure is the mosaic of the Madonna in the half-dome of the central apse. Starkly set on a pure gold background, the figure is one of the most stunning works of Byzantine art you will see in Italy.

It is also possible to climb the **bell tower**, from which you'll be greeted by great views across the island and lagoon.

DON'T MISS • Chiesa di Santa Fosca • Palazzo del Consiglio

sights & activities

It barely seems possible that so much could have been packed into the 7.6 sq km that make up Venice. Few people do more than scratch the surface over a couple of days, but Venice could have you walking in circles for months and you'd still not feel you had the hang of it.

Churches of every size and description festoon the city. You can marvel at the tiny marble Renaissance gem of **Santa Maria dei Miracoli** (p. 46) or be awestruck by the Palladian magnificence of **San Francesco della Vigna** (p. 44).

A handful of grand mansions allows you to get an idea of how the aristocrats of La Serenissima lived and to take in modest (extra) doses of art and period furnishings at the same time. **Palazzo Querini-Stampaglia** (p. 38) and **Ca' Rezzonico** (p. 38) are good examples. Most of Venice, however, forms a vast artistic wonderland. Countless fine buildings can be admired from the outside, and occasionally from within. You really never know when you might bump into something such as the remarkable spiral stairway of the **Palazzo Contarini del Bovolo** (p. 40) or one of the grand religious confraternities, such as the **Scuola Grande di San Marco** (p. 42).

The more you look the more you'll see, from **squeri** (gondola repair yards) to the intriguing freshwater **wells** all over the city, from half-hidden parks to impossibly narrow **calli** (streets).

Venice Card

Introduced in 2001, the Venice Card offers combined transport, attraction and amenities costs. Blue tickets include public toilets and the Casino (for adults), while orange tickets allow entry to the Musei Civici (Civic Museums; see also Special Tickets p. 14). The cost (€5.70-50.10) depends on your age and duration of the ticket. You can also include the boat service from the airport or a discounted parking rate. You must book 48 hours in advance of arrival (within Italy ☎ 899 90 90 90, from abroad ☎ 00 39 041 271 47 47, @ www.venicecard.it). The only serious savings you are likely to make, however, will be on frequent use of the public amenities!

Damien Simonis

Off the Beaten Track

It is possible to explore lesser known pockets of Venice in comparative peace.

Chug across to **Giudecca**, where the **Chiesa del SS Redentore** (p. 47) can be used as a cultural 'excuse' to wander around this intriguing residential island. Or get down to **Via G Garibaldi** in Castello, a broad and busy boulevard with few sights, but a chirpy local feel, then take a break in the shady **Giardini Pubblici** (p. 54). The back canals of Dorsoduro, Cannaregio and Santa Croce are generally quiet and invite the curious to explore.

MUSEUMS & GALLERIES

Admission to some museums is free for EU citizens under 18 and over 65.

Ca' Pesaro – Galleria d'Arte Moderna (3, A8)

Started by Longhena and completed in 1710 by Gaspari, this Baroque mansion is considered one of the most important on the Grand Canal. Since 1902 it has housed the Galleria d'Arte Moderna, a broad collection, including pieces by de Chirico, Miró, Chagall, Kandinsky, Klee, Klimt, Moore and others. It was closed in the early 1980s for restoration.
✉ Fondamenta de Ca' Pesaro, Santa Croce 2076 ☎ 041 524 06 95 🚊 San Stae: Nos 1 & N ⏰ opens in late 2002

A Modern Touch

Carlo Scarpa (1906-78) was Venice's best known modern architect. Designer of the IUAV, the city's prestigious architectural university, Scarpa was given the task of lending a modern touch to various interiors of Venice's great buildings, including the Palazzo Querini-Stampaglia, Museo Correr and the Gallerie dell'Accademia.

Ca' Pesaro – Museo d'Arte Orientale (3, A8)

Also in Ca' Pesaro, on the top floor, the Oriental Art Museum features Asian and Eastern oddments, including important collections of Edo-period art from Japan, and Chinese porcelain.
✉ Fondamenta de Ca' Pesaro, Santa Croce 2076

☎ 041 524 11 73 🚊 San Stae: Nos 1 & N ⏰ Tues-Sun 8.15am-2pm ⓢ €2.10

Ca' Rezzonico – Museo del Settecento Veneziano (3, H5)

Designed by Longhena and completed in the 1750s, this magnificent mansion houses a collection of 18th century art (including some fine ceiling frescoes by Tiepolo) and furniture. It is also worth visiting for the views over the Grand Canal. The Salone da Ballo (Ballroom) is a splendid hall dripping with frescoes and is richly furnished with 18th century couches, tables and statues in ebony.
✉ Fondamenta Rezzonico, Dorsoduro 3136 ☎ 041 241 01 00 🚊 Ca' Rezzonico: No 1 ⏰ Wed-Mon 10am-6pm ⓢ €6.75 ♿ limited

Museo della Fondazione Querini-Stampalia (3, E14)

The inside of this *palazzo* (palace) features some surprising modern touches by the Venetian architect Carlo Scarpa. The museum, on the 2nd floor, contains furniture, personal effects and mostly minor art held by the Querini family. Look out for Giovanni Bellini's *Presentazione di Gesù al Tempio* (Presentation of Jesus at the Temple) and Gabriele Bella's curious scenes of Venetian life.
✉ Ponte Querini, Castello 4778 ☎ 041 271 14 11 🚊 San Zaccaria: Nos 1, 6, 14, 41, 42, 51, 52, 71, 72, 82 & N

⏰ Oct-Apr: Tues-Sun 10am-1pm & 3-6pm; May-Sept: Tues-Thurs & Sun 10am-1pm & 3-6pm, Fri-Sat 10am-1pm & 3-10pm ⓢ €6.20 ♿ limited

Museo delle Icone (2, G10)

Attached to the Chiesa di San Giorgio dei Greci (p. 44), this gallery is dedicated to Orthodox religious art. On display are some 80 works of art and a series of other items. Foremost are two 14th century Byzantine icons, one representing Christ in Glory and the other the Virgin Mary with Child and Apostles. Many items were created by Greeks in Venice and northern Italy.
✉ Ponte dei Greci, Castello 3412 ☎ 041 522 65 81 🚊 San Zaccaria: Nos 1, 6, 14, 41, 42, 51, 52, 71, 72, 82 & N ⏰ Mon-Sat 9am-12.30pm & 2-4.30pm, Sun 10am-5pm ⓢ €3.65

Museo Diocesano d'Arte Sacra (3, G14)

The most interesting element of this religious art museum is the charming Romanesque cloister, a rarity in Venice and often open longer hours than the art display itself, which is housed in a former Benedictine monastery dedicated to Sant' Apollonia.
✉ Fondamenta di Sant'Apollonia, Castello 4312 ☎ 041 522 91 66 🚊 San Zaccaria: Nos 1, 6, 14, 41, 42, 51, 52,

71, 72, 82 & N
🕐 Mon-Sat 10.30am-12.30pm ⑤ voluntary contribution

Museo Storico Navale (2, G11)
Spread over four floors in a former grain silo, this museum traces the maritime history of the city and of Italy. Models abound of everything from the *bucintoro* (the doges' ceremonial barge) to WWII battleships. Up on the 3rd floor is a room containing a few gondolas, including Peggy Guggenheim's.
✉ **Fondamenta dell'Arsenale, Castello 2148** ☎ 041 520 02 76
🚇 **Arsenale: Nos 1, 41 & 42** 🕐 **Mon-Fri 8.45am-1pm, Sat 8.45am-1.30pm**
⑤ €1.55

Palazzo Fortuny
(3, F9) Sporting two rows of *hectafores*, each a series of eight connected Venetian-style windows, this mansion was bought by Mariano Fortuny y Madrazo, an eccentric Spanish painter and collector, in the early 20th century. His works, and another 80 by the Roman artist Virgilio Guidi, make up the display.
✉ **Campo San Beneto, San Marco 3780**
☎ **041 520 09 95**
🇪 **www.comune .venezia.it/museicivici**
🚇 **Sant'Angelo: Nos 1 & 82** 🕐 **opens in 2004**

NOTABLE BUILDINGS & MONUMENTS

Ateneo Veneto
(3, H10) This learned society, founded in Napoleon's time, was once the headquarters of the confraternity of San Girolamo and Santa Maria della Giustizia, whose main task was to accompany criminals on death row in their last moments. The building was known as the Scuola 'dei Picai' (the old Venetian version of Dead Men Walking).
✉ **Campo San Fantin, San Marco** 🚇 **Vallaresso & San Marco: Nos 1, 3, 4, 82 & N** ♿ limited

Dogana da Mar
(3, K11) The customs offices that long occupied the low slung Dogana have gone and nothing has replaced them. The Punta della Dogana marks the split between the Grand Canal and the Canale della Giudecca. Atop the Dogana da Mar buildings are two bronze Atlases and, above them, turns capricious Fortune, an elaborate weather vane.
✉ **Punta della Dogana, Dorsoduro 10** 🚇 **Salute: No 1** ♿ good

Bartolomeo Colleoni Statue (3, C15)
Presiding over the Campo SS Giovanni e Paolo is the most impressive of the city's two equestrian statues. It was created by the Florentine Verrocchio (1435-88) and is dedicated to the *condottiero* (professional mercenary commander) Bartolomeo Colleoni, who from 1448 commanded mercenary armies in the name of the Republic.
✉ **Campo SS Giovanni e Paolo, Castello**
🚇 **Ospedale Civile: Nos 41, 42, 51 & 52**

Verrocchio's Bartolomeo

A Mercenary Moved
When freewheeling mercenary Bartolomeo Colleoni died in 1474, he bequeathed 216,000 gold and silver ducats and considerably more in property to his former employer, the city of Venice, on condition that a statue to him be raised in St Mark's Square. Venice took the money and also raised the statue, a masterpiece as it happens, but could not stomach the idea of having it in the city's main square. Instead La Serenissima opted to place it in Campo SS Giovanni e Paolo, which after all, is fronted by the Scuola Grande di *San Marco*!

Arsenale (2, G12)

Venice's huge dockyards were founded in 1104 and churned out warships and merchantmen on an industrial scale. The area is still navy property and you can only enter the vestibule at the land entrance, which is surmounted by the lion of St Mark, and peer through.
✉ Campo de l'Arsenal, Castello 2407 🚊 Arsenale: Nos 1, 41 & 42 ⏰ about 7am-5pm (when open to navy staff)

Ca' Foscari (3, G5)

This late-Gothic structure was commissioned by Doge Francesco Foscari and is now the seat of the university. Although one of the finest mansions in the city, it has fallen into disrepair. In mid-1999 a deceptively realistic mock facade was unveiled to hide restoration work that is still underway.
✉ Campiello de Ca' Foscari, Dorsoduro 3246 🚊 San Tomà: Nos 1, 82 & N

Campanile (3, G13)

St Mark's Basilica's 99m-tall bell tower was raised in the 10th century but suddenly collapsed on 14 July 1902 and had to be rebuilt brick by brick. Oddly, it contains just one bell, the *marangona*, which survived the fall. You take a lift to the top, from where there are views across the entire city.
✉ Piazza San Marco, San Marco 🚊 Vallaresso, San Marco & San Zaccaria: Nos 1, 3, 4, 6, 14, 41, 42, 51, 52, 71, 72, 82 & N ⏰ late June-Aug: 9am-9pm; Apr-June & Sept-Oct:

9am-7pm; Nov-Mar: 9.30am-5.30pm
⑤ €5.20

Casa di Goldoni

(3, F6) Venice's greatest playwright, Carlo Goldoni (1707-93) was born in the Palazzo Centani, now known better as his house. It has been opened up as a museum, although there is little to see but some 18th century marionettes and a series of images of, and commentaries on, the playwright (in Italian only). The house is worth a look though if you have purchased a combined ticket.
✉ Calle Nomboli 2794, San Polo ☎ 041 523 63 53 🚊 San Tomà: Nos 1, 82 & N ⏰ Apr-Oct: Mon-Sat 10am-5pm; Nov-Mar: Mon-Sat 10am-4pm ⑤ €2.60

Fondaco dei Tedeschi

(3, D12) From the 13th century, the German business community occupied this fondaco *(fontego)*, or trading house. The present building was raised after a fire in 1505, and decorated by Giorgione and Titian (see also Ca' d'Oro p. 22). The courtyard was covered in 1937 and the building now serves as a post office.
✉ Salizzada del

Fondaco dei Tedeschi, San Marco 5554
🚊 Rialto: Nos 1, 4, 82 & N ⏰ Mon-Sat 8.10am-7pm ♿ limited

Fondaco dei Turchi

(3, A7) See p. 54.

Ospedaletto (2, E10)

Longhena's 17th century 'Little Hospital' (aka Chiesa di Santa Maria dei Derelitti) was the focal point of a hospital for elderly and poor patients. It remains one of the gaudiest displays of Baroque in Venice. In an annexe is the elegantly frescoed Sala da Musica, where patients performed concerts.
✉ Barbaria delle Tole, Castello 6691 ☎ 041 270 24 64 🚊 Ospedale Civile: Nos 41, 42, 51 & 52 ⏰ Thurs-Sat 3.30-6.30pm ⑤ €1.55 (Sala da Musica)

Palazzo Contarini del Bovolo (3, G10)

Built in the late 15th century, the Contarini mansion is nicknamed after its dizzying external spiral (*bovolo* in the Venetian dialect) staircase. The building maintains a hint of the Gothic in its arches and capitals. You can enter the grounds if you wish,

As Scary as Hell

At its peak the Arsenale covered 46 hectares, was home to 300 shipping companies and employed 16,000 people. In 1570 the Arsenale put out an astounding 100 galleys in just two months to equip an emergency fleet. The following year at the Battle of Lepanto more than half the allied Christian fleet (which included Imperial Spain) was provided by Venice. Centuries earlier, Dante was so awestruck by the shipyards that he used them as a model for his vision of hell in his *Divina Commedia* (Canto XXI, 7-21).

although the staircase is quite visible from outside.
✉ **Calle Contarini del Bovolo, San Marco 4299** ☎ **041 270 24 64**
🚤 **Rialto: Nos 1, 4, 82 & N** 🕐 **10am-6pm**
💲 **€2.10** ♿ **limited**

Palazzo Corner (Ca' Grande) (3, J8)

Sansovino's 16th century masterpiece of residential building was built for Jacopo Corner, a nephew of the ill-fated Caterina, the queen of Cyprus, and now houses the provincial prefecture. You can only admire it from the Grand Canal.
✉ **San Marco 2662**
🚤 **Santa Maria del Giglio: No 1**

Palazzo Dario (3, K9)

The best way to appreciate this palazzo is from the No 1 vaporetto – the unique Renaissance marble facing was taken down and then later reattached in the 19th century.
✉ **Calle Barbaro, Dorsoduro 352**
🚤 **Salute: No 1**

Sightseeing on the No 1

Palazzo Labia (4, D4)

Nowadays home to the RAI, Italy's national broadcaster, this fine 17th century mansion boasts interesting Tiepolo frescoes inside.
✉ **Campo San Geremia, Cannaregio 275** ☎ **041 78 12 77** 🚤 **Ferrovia: Nos 1, 3, 4, 41, 42, 51, 52, 71, 72, 82 & N**
🕐 **Wed-Fri 3-4pm (call ahead to book)** 💲 **free** ♿ **limited**

Palazzo Loredan & Ca' Farsetti (3, E10)

These started life in the 12th century as *fondachi*, family houses whose ground floor served as warehouses. In 1826 the town hall moved to the Ca' Farsetti from the Doge's Palace. Forty-two years later it acquired Palazzo Loredan. You can wander into the foyer of the latter.
✉ **Riva del Carbon, San Marco 4136-4137** 🚤 **Rialto: Nos 1, 4, 82 & N**

Palazzo Mocenigo (3, B7)

Once the property of one of the Republic's most important families, the mansion now houses a modest museum featuring period clothes, furnishings and accessories of the 18th century. This is how the other half lived in the twilight years of

La Serenissima.
✉ **Salizzada di San Stae, Santa Croce 1992**
☎ **041 721 17 98**
🚤 **San Stae: Nos 1 & N**
🕐 **Tues-Sun 10am-5pm**
💲 **€4.15**

Palazzo Vendramin-Calergi (4, E7)

Gamblers approaching by water taxi *(motoscafo)* are greeted by the restrained Renaissance facade of what is now home to the city casino (see also p. 100). The composer Richard Wagner died here in 1883. You can wander into the ground floor area but pay to see the gaming rooms.
✉ **Campiello Vendramin, Cannaregio 2040**
☎ **041 529 71 11**
🌐 **www.casinovenezia .it** 🚤 **San Marcuola: Nos 1, 82 & N** 🕐 **Oct-May 3pm-3am** 💲 **€2.60 (gaming rooms)** ♿ **limited**

Scuola di San Giorgio degli Schiavoni (2, F10)

Venice's Dalmatian community established this religious school in the 15th century. On the ground floor the walls are graced by a series of superb paintings by Vittore Carpaccio depicting events in the lives of the three patron saints of Dalmatia: George, Tryphone and Jerome.

Blind Revenge

Just left of Bar Omnibus is the narrow Gothic 14th century Palazzo Dandolo, Riva del Carbon, San Marco 4172 (3, E10). The house belonged to blind doge Enrico Dandolo, who led the Fourth Crusade to a famous (if treacherous) victory over Constantinople in 1204. Considered by many Venetians the greatest doge ever, Dandolo by his actions helped sow the seeds of the Byzantine Empire's destruction.

The image of St George dispatching the dragon to the next life is particularly graphic.

✉ **Calle dei Furlani, Castello 3259/a**
☎ **041 522 88 28**
🚤 **San Zaccaria: Nos 1, 6, 14, 20, 41, 42, 51, 52, 71, 72, 82 & N** ⏰ **Tues-Sat 9.30am-12.30pm & 3.30-6.30pm, Sun 9.30am-12.30pm** 💲 **€2.60** ♿ **limited**

Scuola Grande dei Carmini (3, G3)

In its heyday, this was probably the most powerful of Venice's religious confraternities, with a membership in 1675 of 75,000. The facades have been attributed to Longhena. Of its numerous works of art, the nine ceiling paintings by Tiepolo in the Salone Superiore (upstairs) depict the virtues surrounding the Virgin in Glory.

✉ **Rio Terrà Canal, Dorsoduro 2617** ☎ **041 528 94 20** 🚤 **Ca' Rezzonico: No 1** ⏰ **Mon-Sat 9am-6pm, Sun 9am-4pm** 💲 **€4.15** ♿ **limited**

Scuola Grande di San Giovanni Evangelista

(3, C5) Behind what seems like an enormous iconostasis off Calle Magazen, two impressive facades give onto a courtyard. On the southern side is the Chiesa di San Giovanni Evangelista, while opposite is one of the six major Venetian *scuole* (see below), dedicated to the same saint. Codussi designed the interior. The sumptuous 1st floor hall dates from 1727.

✉ **Campiello della Scuola, San Polo 2454** ☎ **041 71 82 34** 🚤 **Ferrovia: Nos 1, 3, 4, 41, 42, 51, 52, 71, 72, 82 & N** ⏰ **by appointment only** 💲 **€2.60** ♿ **limited**

Scuola Grande di San Marco (3, C15)

At right angles to the Chiesa dei SS Giovanni e Paolo (p. 35), the eye-catching marble facade of this former religious confraternity is a Renaissance gem. Apart from the magnificent lions, you will notice the sculpted trompe l'oeil perspectives covering much of the lower half of the facade. Nowadays the scuola is the entrance (you are free to wander in) to the Ospedale Civile.

✉ **Campo SS Giovanni e Paolo, Castello** 🚤 **Ospedale Civile: Nos 41, 42, 51 & 52** ♿ **limited**

Torre dell'Orologio

(3, G13) Two thickset Moors (Mori) strike the hour on this emblematic clock tower, built at the end of the 15th century. At certain times of the year (such as during Ascension Week) models of the Wise Men come out and bow to an image of the Madonna above them.

✉ **Piazza San Marco, San Marco** 🚤 **Vallaresso, San Marco & San Zaccaria: Nos 1, 3, 4, 6, 14, 41, 42, 51, 52, 71, 72, 82 & N**

When School Was Cool

In a world without a welfare state, lay religious confraternities under a patron saint formed 'schools' *(scuole)* which served as community associations.

The 15th century saw the division between the big six (the Scuole Grandi – dedicated to San Marco, San Rocco, San Teodoro, San Giovanni Evangelista, Santa Maria della Misericordia and Santa Maria della Carità) and the rest (the Scuole Minori; totalling about 400). Most workers' and artisans' guilds had a *scuola*. As club, welfare centre and rallying point for parades and religious events, they formed (with the parish church) the backbone of society.

CHURCHES & CATHEDRALS

Carmini (3, H2)
What remains of the original 14th century Byzantine and then Gothic Chiesa dei Carmini sits a little uneasily side by side with the richer, and perhaps less digestible, ornament of the 16th and 17th centuries. Among the paintings on view are several works by Cima da Conegliano.
✉ **Campo dei Carmini, Dorsoduro 2614**
☎ **041 522 65 53**
🚤 **Ca' Rezzonico: No 1; or San Basilio: Nos 61, 62, 82 & N** ⏱ **Mon-Sat 7.30am-noon & 2.30-7.10pm, Sun 7.30am-noon & 2.30-4.30pm**
⑤ **free** ♿ **limited**

Cattedrale di San Pietro di Castello
(2, G14) This isolated post-Palladian cathedral, with the gleaming but leaning bell tower, is the latest successor to a line of churches that have stood here since a bishopric was created on the island of San Pietro in 775. Although Venice's cathedral until 1807, it had for centuries been bridesmaid to St Mark's Basilica.
✉ **Isola di San Pietro, Castello** ☎ **041 275 04 62** 🄴 **www.provincia.venezia.it/chorus**
🚤 **San Pietro: Nos 51 & 52** ⏱ **Mon-Sat 10am-5pm, Sun 1-5pm**
⑤ **€1.55**

Gesuati (2, H6)
Also known as the Chiesa di Santa Maria del Rosario, this 18th century Dominican church contains ceiling frescoes by Tiepolo telling the story of St Dominic. The statues lining the interior are by Gian Maria

Morlaiter (1699-1781).
✉ **Fondamenta Zattere ai Gesuati, Dorsoduro 918** ☎ **041 523 06 25**
🚤 **Zattere: Nos 51, 52, 61, 62, 82 & N** ⏱ **8am-noon & 5-7pm** ⑤ **€1.55**
♿ **limited**

I Gesuiti (2, D9)
The Jesuits took over this church in 1657 and reconstructed it in Roman Baroque style. Inside the lavish decor includes white and gold stucco, white and green marble floors and marble flourishes filling empty slots. Remarkable paintings found here are Tintoretto's *Assunzione della Vergine* (Assumption of the Virgin), in the north transept, and Titian's *Martirio di San Lorenzo* (Martyrdom of St Lawrence).
✉ **Campo dei Gesuiti, Cannaregio 4884**
☎ **041 528 65 79**
🚤 **Fondamente Nuove: Nos 12, 13, 41, 42, 51 & 52** ⏱ **10am-noon & 4-6pm** ⑤ **free** ♿ **limited**

San Giacomo dell'Orio (3, B6)
Replacing a 9th century church (in 1225), this is one of the few decent examples of Romanesque in Venice. The main Gothic addition (14th century) is the remarkable wooden ceiling. Among the intriguing jumble inside you'll find a 13th century baptismal font, a Byzantine column in green marble and a rare work by Lorenzo Lotto, *Madonna col Bambino e Santi* (Madonna with Child and Saints).
✉ **Campo di San Giacomo dell'Orio, Santa Croce** ☎ **041 275 04 62**

🄴 **www.provincia.venezia.it/chorus**
🚤 **Riva de Biasio: No 1** ⏱ **Mon-Sat 10am-5pm, Sun 1-5pm** ⑤ **€1.55**
♿ **limited**

San Sebastiano (3, J1)
What you see here is the Renaissance reconstruction of Paolo Veronese's parish church. Veronese decorated the inside with frescoes and canvases that cover much of the ceiling and walls. The organ is his work too, with scenes from Christ's life on its shutters. Titian contributed his *San Nicolò*, on the right as soon as you enter.
✉ **Campo San Sebastiano, Dorsoduro**
☎ **041 275 04 62**
🚤 **San Basilio: Nos 61, 62, 82 & N** 🄴 **www.provincia.venezia.it/chorus** ⏱ **Mon-Sat 10am-5pm, Sun 3-5pm**
⑤ **€1.55** ♿ **limited**

Fresco-full San Sebastiano

Damien Simonis

Madonna dell'Orto's facade

Madonna dell'Orto

(4, A9) This 14th century church was raised after a statue of the Virgin Mary was discovered by 'miracle' in a nearby garden. Mostly Gothic, the church preserves some Romanesque touches as well as later changes. The five statues crowning the facade were actually added in the 18th century. You'll find the famous white stone Madonna statue in the Cappella di San Mauro.

✉ **Campo della Madonna dell'Orto, Cannaregio 3520**
☎ **041 275 04 62**
e www.provincia .venezia.it/chorus
🚊 Madonna dell'Orto: Nos 41, 42, 51 & 52
🕐 **Mon-Sat 10am-5pm, Sun 1-5pm** 💲 **€1.55**
♿ limited

San Cassiano (3, B9)

Three of Tintoretto's paintings decorate the sanctuary of this church: the *Crocifissione* (Crucifixion), the *Risurrezione* (Resurrection) and the *Discesa al Limbo* (Descent into Limbo).
✉ **Campo San Cassiano,**

San Polo ☎ 041 72 14 08 🚊 San Stae: Nos 1 & N 🕐 Tues-Sat 9am-noon 💲 free ♿ limited

San Francesco della Vigna (2, F11)

The first glimpse of this powerful Palladian facade comes as a shock. The church itself was designed by Sansovino for the Franciscans on the site of a vineyard. The bell tower could be the twin of St Mark's Campanile. Inside, the Cappella dei Giustiniani, left of the main altar, is decorated with splendid reliefs by Pietro Lombardo and his school.
✉ **Campo San Francesco della Vigna, Castello 2787**

☎ 041 520 61 02 🚊 Celestia: Nos 41, 42, 51 & 52 🕐 8am-12.30pm & 3-7pm 💲 free ♿ limited

San Giorgio dei Greci

(2, G10) Here in 1526 Greek Orthodox refugees were allowed to raise a church. It is interesting for the richness of its Byzantine icons, iconostasis and other works inside. Visit the Museo delle Icone next door (p. 38).
✉ **Ponte dei Greci, Castello 3412** ☎ **041 522 54 46** 🚊 **San Zaccaria: Nos 1, 6, 14, 41, 42, 51, 52, 71, 72, 82 & N** 🕐 **Mon & Wed-Sat 9am-1pm & 3-4.30pm, Sun 9am-1pm** 💲 **free**

Tintoretto Treasure

A big draw at the Chiesa della Madonna dell'Orto are the frescoes by Tintoretto, who was a local parishioner. Among them are the *Giudizio Finale* (Last Judgment), *Adorazione del Vitello d'Oro* (Adoration of the Golden Calf) and the *Apparizione della Croce a San Pietro* (St Peter's Vision of the Cross). On the wall at the end of the right aisle is the *Presentazione di Maria al Tempio* (Presentation of the Virgin Mary in the Temple). Tintoretto is buried with other family members in the church.

Detail of the 14th century Madonna dell'Orto

San Giovanni Crisostomo (3, C12)

Since 1977 this church (which was remodelled in 1504 on a Greek cross plan) has housed an icon of the Virgin Mary that attracts many of the faithful. To wander in is to feel yourself transported to a mysterious church of the Orthodox East.

✉ **Campo San Giovanni Crisostomo, Cannaregio 5890 ☎ 041 522 71 55** 🚤 **Rialto: Nos 1, 4, 82 & N** ⏲ **Mon-Sat 8.15am-12.15pm & 3-7pm, Sun & hols 10.15am-12.15pm & 3-7pm** ⑤ **free**

San Nicolò dei Mendicoli (2, G3)

The portico, attached to one side of this 13th century church, was used to shelter the poor in a district known for its *mendicoli* (beggars). On the tiny square, bounded in by the canals, is a pylon bearing a weatherworn winged lion of St Mark (one of the few not to be destroyed under Napoleon and later restored).

✉ **Campo San Nicolò dei Mendicoli, Dorsoduro 1839 ☎ 041 528 59 52** 🚤 **San Basilio: Nos 61, 62, 82 & N** ⏲ **Mon-Sat 10am-noon & 4-5.30pm, Sun 4-6pm** ⑤ **free**

San Pantalon (3, F4)

Behind the cracked 17th century facade of this church is an impressive series of 40 canvases representing the *Martirio e Gloria di San Pantaleone* (Martyrdom and Glory of St Pantaleone) painted for the ceiling by Giovanni Antonio Fumiani. Veronese, Vivarini and Palma il Giovane also contributed.

✉ **Campo San Pantalon,**

Dorsoduro 3670 ☎ 041 523 58 93 🚤 **San Tomà: Nos 1, 82 & N** ⏲ **Mon-Sat 4-6pm** ⑤ **free** ♿ **limited**

San Polo (3, E7)

Largely obscured by the housing tacked onto it, you'd never know this church is of Byzantine origin. Inside, a whole cycle by Tiepolo, the *Via Crucis* (Stations of the Cross), has been stacked rather unceremoniously along the walls of the sacristy.

✉ **Campo San Polo, San Polo 2118 ☎ 041 275 04 62** 📧 **www.provincia .venezia.it/chorus** 🚤 **San Silvestro: No 1** ⏲ **Mon-Sat 10am-5pm, Sun 1-5pm** ⑤ **€1.55** ♿ **limited**

San Rocco (3, E4)

If you're not already tired of all the art, behind the 18th century Baroque facade of this church, squatting virtually opposite the Scuola Grande di San Rocco (p. 34), you can inspect a mixed bag inside, including a few more Tintorettos.

✉ **Campo San Rocco, Dorsoduro 3053 ☎ 041 523 48 64** 🚤 **San Tomà: Nos 1, 82 & N** ⏲ **7.30am-12.30pm & 3-5pm** ⑤ **free**

San Salvador (3, E12)

Built on a plan of three Greek crosses laid end to end, this church is among the city's oldest, although the present facade was erected in 1663. Among the noteworthy works inside is Titian's *Annunciazione* (Annunciation). Behind the main altar is his *Trasfigurazione*

(Transfiguration).

✉ **Campo San Salvador, San Marco ☎ 041 523 67 17** 🚤 **Rialto: Nos 1, 4, 82 & N** ⏲ **Mon-Sat 10am-noon & 3-6pm** ⑤ **free** ♿ **limited**

San Stae (3, A8)

The busy Baroque facade of this church dedicated to St Eustace (San Stae) belies the simple interior. Among its art treasures are Tiepolo's *Il Martirio di San Bartolomeo* (The Martyrdom of St Bartholomew). Next door, to the left (No 1980), is the **Scuola dei Tiraoro e Battioro**, the former seat of the goldsmith confraternity's scuola.

✉ **Campo San Stae, Santa Croce 1979 ☎ 041 275 04 62** 📧 **www.provincia .venezia.it/chorus** 🚤 **San Stae: Nos 1 & N** ⏲ **Mon-Sat 10am-5pm, Sun 1-5pm** ⑤ **€1.55** ♿ **limited**

San Trovaso (3, K5)

This church was rebuilt in the 16th century on the site of its 9th century predecessor. The associated scuola was home to the confraternity of squerarioli (gondola builders). Inside the church are a couple of Tintorettos.

✉ **Campo San Trovaso, Dorsoduro ☎ 041 522 21 33** 🚤 **Zattere: Nos 51, 52, 61, 62, 82 & N** ⏲ **Mon-Sat 8-11am & 3.30-6.30pm, Sun 8.30am-noon** ⑤ **free** ♿ **limited**

San Zaccaria (2, G10)

Construction of this church started in Gothic (see the apses) but ended in Renaissance. On the second altar to the left after you

Santa Maria dei Miracoli's stunning shell

Damien Simonis

enter is a startlingly vivid image of the Virgin Mary by Giovanni Bellini. The Cappella di Sant'Atanasio holds some Tintorettos and Tiepolos. The vaults of the Cappella di San Tarasion are covered in frescoes.

✉ **Campo San Zaccaria, Castello 4693** ☎ **041 522 12 57** 🔊 San Zaccaria: Nos 1, 6, 14, 41, 42, 51, 52, 71, 72, 82 & N ◷ 10am-noon & 4-6pm ⑤ free; Cappella di Sant'Atanasio €1.05 ⑤ limited

San Zulian (3, F13)

Supposedly founded in 829, this church, in its actual form (covered in a layer of Istrian stone) was designed by Sansovino. Inside are a few works by Palma il Giovane.

✉ **Campo San Zulian, San Marco** ☎ **041 523 53 83** 🔊 Rialto: Nos 1, 4, 82 & N ◷ Mass: 9.30am, 11am, 7pm ⑤ free

Santa Croce degli Armeni (3, F12)

On Sundays only, Armenian priests from San Lazzaro degli Armeni (p. 50) celebrate a service in this little church, which has been active since at least the 14th century.

✉ **Calle dei Armeni,**

San Marco 956/b 🔊 Vallaresso, San Marco & San Zaccaria: Nos 1, 3, 4, 6, 14, 41, 42, 51, 52, 71, 72, 82 & N ◷ Sun & hols 11am ⑤ free

Santa Maria dei Miracoli (3, C13)

And well might one speak of miracles *(miracoli)*. Pietro Lombardo was responsible for this Renaissance jewel, which is fully carapaced inside and out in marble, bas-reliefs and statues. The timber ceiling is also eye-catching. Pietro and Tullio Lombardo executed the carvings on the choir.

✉ **Campo dei Miracoli, Cannaregio 6074** ☎ **041 275 04 62** e **www.provincia .venezia.it/chorus** 🔊 Rialto: Nos 1, 4, 82 & N ◷ Mon-Sat 10am-5pm, Sun 1-5pm ⑤ €1.55 ⑤ limited

Santa Maria del Giglio (3, J9)

The Baroque facade of this place (aka Santa Maria Zobenigo) features maps of European cities and hides the fact that a church has stood here since the 10th century. A small affair, it is jammed with paintings,

such as Peter Paul Rubens' *Madonna col Bambino e San Giovanni* (his only work in Venice). Behind the altar lurk Tintoretto's moody depictions of the four Evangelists.

✉ **Campo Santa Maria Zobenigo, San Marco 2543** ☎ **041 275 04 62** e **www.provincia .venezia.it/chorus** 🔊 Santa Maria del Giglio: No 1 ◷ Mon-Sat 10am-5pm, Sun 1-5pm ⑤ €1.55 ⑤ limited

Santa Maria della Visitazione (2, H6)

This little-visited church has a curious 15th century chequerboard timber ceiling bearing row upon row of scenes depicting the Visitation and a series of portraits of saints and prophets.

✉ **Fondamenta Zattere ai Gesuati, Dorsoduro 920** ☎ **041 522 40 77** 🔊 Zattere: Nos 51, 52, 61, 62, 82 & N ◷ 8am-12.30pm & 3-7pm ⑤ free ⑤ limited

Santa Maria Formosa (3, E14)

Rebuilt in 1492 on the site of a 7th century church, the name Santa Maria Formosa stems from the legend behind the church's initial foundation. San Magno, bishop of Oderzo, is said to have had a vision of the Virgin Mary on this spot. In this instance she was *formosa* (beautiful, curvy). Inside is an altarpiece by Palma il Vecchio depicting St Barbara.

✉ **Campo Santa Maria Formosa, Castello 5254** ☎ **041 523 46 45** e **www.provincia .venezia.it/chorus** 🔊 San Zaccaria: Nos 1, 6, 14, 41, 42, 51, 52, 71,

72, 82 & N ⊘ Mon-Sat
10am-5pm, Sun 1-5pm
ⓢ €1.55 ⓓ limited

Sant'Alvise (2, C7)
Built in 1388, this church
hosts a noteworthy Tiepolo,
the *Salita al Calvario* (Climb
to Calvary), a distressingly
human depiction of one of
Christ's falls under the
weight of the cross. The ceiling frescoes are an unex-
pected riot of colour.
✉ Campo Sant'Alvise,
Cannaregio 3205
☎ 041 275 04 62
ⓔ www.provincia
.venezia.it/chorus
⚲ Sant'Alvise: Nos 41,
42, 51 & 52 ⊘ Mon-Sat
10am-5pm, Sun 1-5pm
ⓢ €1.55 ⓓ limited

Santo Stefano (3, H8)
One of only three churches
in Venice to have been
attached to a convent,
Santo Stefano boasts the
finest timber ceiling of any
church in Venice. In the
museum right of the
altar is a collection of
Tintorettos, including the
Ultima Cena (Last Supper)
and *Lavanda dei Piedi*
(Washing of the Feet).
The bell tower has a ser-
ious lean.
✉ Campo Santo
Stefano, San Marco
3825 ☎ 041 522 23 62
ⓔ www.provincia
.venezia.it/chorus
⚲ Accademia: Nos 1,
3, 4, 82 & N ⊘ Mon-
Sat 10am-5pm, Sun 1-
5pm ⓢ free; museum
€1.55 ⓓ limited

Scalzi (3, A2)
This Carmelite church of
the barefoot Carmelites
stands out for its ebullient
Baroque facade, in keeping
with the heady Roman
style. The theme continues

inside, where you can also
observe damaged frescoes
by Tiepolo in the vaults of
two of the side chapels.
✉ Fondamenta dei
Scalzi, Cannaregio 56
⚲ Ferrovia: Nos 1, 3,
4, 41, 42, 51, 52, 71,
72, 82 & N ⊘ Mon-Sat
7-11.45am & 4-6.45pm,
Sun & hols 7.45am-
12.30pm & 4-7pm
ⓢ free ⓓ limited

Spirito Santo (2, J7)
The modest Renaissance
facade of this small church
is not overly remarkable.
Boats are lined up from
here to create a bridge
across the Canale della
Giudecca for the Festa del
Redentore in July (see
below and p. 93).
✉ Fondamenta Zattere
allo Spirito Santo,
Dorsoduro 400
⚲ Zattere: Nos 51, 52,
61, 62, 82 & N

SS Apostoli (3, B12)
This church is worth a
quick visit for the 15th
century Cappella Corner by
Mauro Codussi, which fea-
tures a painting of Santa
Lucia by Tiepolo.
✉ Campo dei SS
Apostoli, Cannaregio
4544 ⚲ Ca' d'Oro: Nos
1 & N ⊘ Mon-Sat 7.30-
11.30am & 5-7pm, Sun

8.30am-noon & 4-6.30pm
ⓢ free ⓓ limited

SS Redentore (2, K7)
The authorities ordered
Palladio to design this
grand church in thanks-
giving for the passing of the
plague in 1577. It was finished by Antonio da Ponte.
Inside are a few works by
Tintoretto, Veronese and
Vivarini, but it is the powerful theatrical facade that
most inspires observers.
✉ Campo del SS
Redentore, Giudecca 94
☎ 041 523 14 15
ⓔ www.provincia
.venezia.it/chorus
⚲ Redentore: Nos 41,
42, 82 & N ⊘ Mon-Sat
10am-5pm, Sun 1-5pm
ⓢ €1.55 ⓓ limited

Zitelle (2, J9)
Designed by Palladio in the
late 16th century, the
Chiesa di Santa Maria della
Presentazione, known as
the Zitelle ('old maids'),
was conceived as a church
and hospice for poor young
women. It is now used as a
conference centre.
✉ Fondamenta delle Zi-
telle, Giudecca 32 ☎ 041
521 74 11 ⚲ Zitelle:
Nos 41, 42, 82 & N
⊘ Fri-Sat 10am-noon
ⓢ free ⓓ limited

Pontoon Pilgrims
On the third Saturday of July each year, a grand pontoon bridge is created from all sorts of boats tied together between the Zattere (from outside Spirito
Santo) and Chiesa del SS Redentore, allowing the citizens of Venice to make a pilgrimage that their fore-
bears first undertook in 1578. Many people hang
about on the boats with friends to party and watch
the fireworks that night. The Festa del Redentore
(Feast of the Redeemer) remains one of the city's
prime celebrations.

BRIDGES, CAMPI & PUBLIC SPACES

Biennale Internazionale d'Arte

(2, H13) The pavilions of the Biennale (p. 93) form a mini-compendium of 20th century architectural thinking. Carlo Scarpa worked often on the Italian Pavilion and built the Venezuelan one (1954). Also look for the Padiglione del Libro (Book Pavilion; 1991), Dutch Pavilion (1954), Austrian Pavilion (1934) and Australian Pavilion (1988).

✉ **Biennale Internazionale d'Arte, Castello** 🚊 **Giardini: Nos 1, 41, 42, 51, 52, 61, 62, 82 & N** ♿ **good**

Campo Manin (3, F10)

At this square's centre stands the proud statue of Daniele Manin, with a lion at his feet. He led the anti-Austrian revolt of 1848-9. The square also boasts a remarkably thoughtless 20th century addition at its eastern end: the Cassa di Risparmio di Venezia bank.

✉ **Campo Manin, San Marco** 🚊 **Rialto: Nos 1, 4, 82 & N** ♿ **limited**

Campo Santa Margherita (3, G3)

A real people's square, this space takes on a truly living air in the afternoon as kids come out to play and the youth of Venice sip *spritzes* (p. 95) at the many bars and cafes. The squat little object at the square's southern end was one of the city's many scuole (see p. 42).

✉ **Campo Santa Margherita, Dorsoduro** 🚊 **Ca' Rezzonico: No 1** ♿ **limited**

An Evening with Veronica

Veronica Franco, one of the city's best remembered courtesans, lived on Campo Santa Maria Formosa. Poet, friend of Tintoretto and lover of France's King Henry III, Miss Franco's costly services ranged from witty discourse to horizontal folk dancing.

Campo Santa Maria Formosa, a truly sexy square

Campo Santa Maria Formosa (3, D14)

One of Venice's most appealing squares, this is full of local life. Among the ageing mansions **Palazzo Vitturi** is a good example of the Veneto-Byzantine style, while the **Palazzi Donà** are a mix of Gothic and late Gothic.

✉ **Campo Santa Maria Formosa, Castello** 🚊 **San Zaccaria: Nos 1, 6, 14, 41, 42, 51, 52, 71, 72, 82 & N** ♿ **limited**

Campo Sant'Angelo (3, G9)

Much of this square is raised, with two wells and a large cistern below. In 1801 the Italian musician Domenico Cimarosa died in the 15th century **Palazzo Duodo**

(No 3584). **Palazzo Gritti**, across the square, was built around the same period.

✉ **Campo Sant'Angelo, San Marco** 🚊 **Sant'Angelo: Nos 1 & 82** ♿ **limited**

Giardini Papadopoli

(3, C1) These gardens, one of the few green spaces open to the public, were a great deal more impressive until 1932, when the Rio Nuovo was slammed through them.

✉ **Fondamenta del Croce, Santa Croce** 🚊 **Piazzale Roma: Nos 1, 4, 41, 42, 51, 52, 61, 62, 71, 72, 82 & N** ⏲ **summer 8am-7.30pm, winter 8am-5.30pm** 💲 **free** ♿ **good**

Mercerie (3, F13)

Since medieval times the lanes that lead from San Salvador to the Torre dell'Orologio and into St Mark's Square have been called *mercerie* (*marzaria* in Venetian dialect), referring to the merchants who traditionally lined this route.
✉ **Mercerie, San Marco** 🚊 **Rialto: Nos 1, 4, 82 & N** ♿ **limited**

Ponte dei Scalzi

(3, A3) This elegant high-arched bridge is the first of the three across the Grand Canal. Built in 1934, it replaced an iron bridge built by the Austrians in 1858.
✉ **Ponte dei Scalzi, Cannaregio/Santa Croce** 🚊 **Ferrovia: Nos 1, 3, 4, 41, 42, 51, 52, 71, 72, 82 & N**

Ponte dell'Accademia

(3, J7) Built in 1930 to replace a 19th century metal structure, the third and last of the Grand Canal bridges, built of timber, was supposed to be a temporary arrangement. From the middle, the views both ways up the Grand Canal are spellbinding.
✉ **Ponte dell'Accademia** 🚊 **Accademia: Nos 1, 3, 4, 82 & N**

Ponte delle Guglie

(4, D5) So-called because of the *guglie* (little obelisks) at either end, this is the main crossing point over the Canale di Cannaregio, and there probably isn't a tourist who doesn't cross it en route between the train station and St Mark's Square.
✉ **Ponte delle Guglie, Cannaregio** 🚊 **Guglie: Nos 41, 42, 51 & 52** ♿ **good**

Ponte di Rialto

(3, D11) For centuries the only bridge over the Grand Canal was here, linking the Rialto with San Marco. Antonio da Ponte (Anthony of the Bridge) completed this robust marble version in 1592, at a cost of 250,000 ducats. It had been preceded by several timber bridges and a wobbly pontoon arrangement as far back as 1180.
✉ **Ponte di Rialto, San Polo/San Marco** 🚊 **Rialto: Nos 1, 4, 82 & N**

Riva degli Schiavoni

(3, H15) Named after Slavs (actually Dalmatians) who in medieval times fished off this waterfront, this became the principal dock for vessels from all over the world. Today it's busy with myriad vessels.
✉ **Riva degli Schiavoni, Castello** 🚊 **San Zaccaria: Nos 1, 6, 14, 41, 42, 51, 52, 71, 72, 82 & N** ♿ **limited**

Sant'Elena (2, J14)

Housing construction began in 1925 in this, the quietest and leafiest residential corner of Venice. The arrival of riot police and armies of football supporters at the **Stadio Penzo** are a bit of a weekend jolt. The humble Gothic **Chiesa di Sant'Elena** is just past the stadium.
✉ **Sant'Elena** 🚊 **Sant' Elena: Nos 1, 41, 42, 51, 52, 61 & 62** ♿ **good**

The Zattere (2, H6)

The Fondamenta Zattere runs the length of the southern side of Dorsoduro along the Canale della Giudecca, and unsurprisingly is a popular spot for the *passeggiata* (an evening or Sunday stroll).
✉ **Fondamenta Zattere, Dorsoduro** 🚊 **Zattere: Nos 51, 52, 61, 62, 82 & N** ♿ **limited**

Damien Simonis

Well, Well, Well

In days gone by Venice had far fewer bridges and no running water, but had an ingenious well system. Nowadays sealed shut, you'll see them in almost every square.

Each well is surrounded by as many as four depressions up to 4m away. Rainwater drained into these depressions and seeped into a cistern below. Sand and/or gravel inside the cistern acted as a filter. In the middle of the cistern, a brick cylinder (the well) extended to the bottom. The cistern itself was sealed off with impenetrable clay to keep salt water out.

MINOR ISLANDS

Le Vignole (5, D8)

The southwestern part of Le Vignole is owned by the military and contains an old fort, the Forte Sant'Andrea, which may only be seen from the sea. The island long produced the bulk of the doge's wine and its 50 or so inhabitants still live mainly from agriculture.

✉ **Le Vignole** ⚓ **Vignole: No 13** ♿ **limited**

Pellestrina (1, D7)

Pellestrina stretches south like an 11km-long razor blade from the Lido to Chioggia. Small villages made up of farming and fishing families are spread out along the island, protected on the seaward side by the Murazzi (sea walls), which are a remarkable feat of 18th century engineering. Long grey sand beaches separate the Murazzi from the sea on calm days.

✉ **Pellestrina** 🚌 **No 11 from Lido** ⚓ **Lido: Nos 1, 6, 14, 20, 51, 52, 61, 62, 82 & N** ♿ **limited**

San Clemente (5, F6) & San Servolo (5, E7)

The Isola di San Clemente was once the site of a hospice for pilgrims returning from the Middle East, and more recently a psychiatric hospital. The Isola di San Servolo shared these latter functions. Until the 17th century Benedictine monks had a monastery here, bits of which remain in the former hospital. The island houses various cultural institutions.

✉ **San Clemente & San Servolo** ⚓ **No 20** ♿ **limited**

San Francesco del Deserto (5, B9)

The Franciscans built a monastery on this island 1km south of Burano to keep away from it all. Legend says Francis of Assisi himself landed here. Malaria and other hardships obliged the Franciscans to leave in 1420. Pope Pius II subsequently granted the island to another order, the **Minori Osservanti**, who remain here (☎ 041 528 68 63; Tues-Sun 9-11am & 3-5pm; donation encouraged).

✉ **San Francesco del Deserto** ⚓ **water taxi from Burano** ♿ **limited**

San Lazzaro degli Armeni (5, F7)

In 1717 the Armenian Mechitarist fathers were handed this former leper colony. They founded a monastery and an important centre of learning.

Visitors can see the 18th century refectory, church, library, museum and art gallery (☎ 041 526 01 04; guided tour only 3.25-5pm; €5.20). A mix of Venetian and Armenian art is on show, along with a room dedicated to Lord Byron, who frequently stayed on the island.

✉ **San Lazzaro degli Armeni** ⚓ **San Lazzaro: No 20** ♿ **limited**

Sant'Erasmo (5, C9)

Together with Le Vignole, Sant'Erasmo was long known as the *orto di Venezia* (Venice's Garden) and its 1000 inhabitants remain largely dedicated to rural pursuits. Apart from green fields and a couple of settlements, you can see the Torre Massimiliana, a 19th century Austrian defensive fort in the southeast.

✉ **Sant'Erasmo** ⚓ **Chiesa: No 13** ♿ **limited**

Chioggia

The most important town in the Comune di Venezia after Venice, and a big fishing port, Chioggia lies to the south of the lagoon (1, D7; ⚓ Lido: Nos 1, 6, 14, 20, 51, 52, 61, 62, 82 & N then 🚌 No 11). Wander along **Corso del Popolo**, visit the **Chiesa di San Domenico** for Vittore Carpaccio's *San Paolo* and check out the fish market. Try to hang about for lunch or dinner too (p. 88).

Check out Chioggia's great-value eateries.

QUIRKY VENICE

Calle del Paradiso

(3, E13) This lane is marked by two Gothic arches. The eastern one, Arco del Paradiso (Heaven's Arch), depicts the Virgin Mary. The lane harks back to a medieval era: shops at street level and jutting out above them on timber barbicans, the upper storeys for offices and living quarters.

✉ **Calle del Paradiso, Castello** 🚣 **Rialto: Nos 1, 4, 82 & N** ♿ limited

Corte del Cavallo

(4, A8) This long courtyard received its name (Horse Court) because the bronze for the great equestrian statue to Colleoni in Campo SS Giovanni e Paolo (p. 39) was melted down here.

✉ **Corte del Cavallo, Cannaregio** 🚣 **Madonna dell'Orto: Nos 41, 42, 51 & 52** ♿ limited

Fondamenta dei Mori

(4, B8) Tintoretto lived at No 3399 on this street. The strange statue of a turbaned man next door on the wall of Palazzo Mastelli is one of four spread out along here and around the corner on Corte dei Mori. These 'Moors' are said to represent the Mastelli family, 12th century merchants from the Morea.

✉ **Fondamenta dei Mori, Cannaregio** 🚣 **Madonna dell'Orto: Nos 41, 42, 51 & 52** ♿ limited

Molino Stucky (2, J4)

Raised in the late 19th century, this was the best known of Giudecca's factories. The windowless brick structure was closed in 1954 and is being restored in a project destined to convert it into a hotel and apartments complex.

✉ **Campiello Priuli, Giudecca 753/c** 🚣 **Sacca Fisola: Nos 41, 42, 82 & N** ♿ limited

Ponte delle Tette

(3, C8) Tits Bridge got its name around the late 15th century because prostitutes around here tended to display their wares to encourage business. Beyond the bridge is Rio Terrà delle Carampane. The name came from a noble family's house (Ca' Rampani), but at some point the ladies of the night here came to be known as *carampane*.

✉ **Ponte delle Tette, San Polo** 🚣 **San Stae: Nos 1 & N**

San Michele (2, C11)

Napoleon established this island cemetery away from the city for health reasons. The Chiesa di San Michele in Isola was among the city's first Renaissance buildings. Ezra Pound, Sergei Diaghilev and Igor Stravinsky are pushing up daisies here, in the 'acatholic' sections (signposted) in the northeast of the island.

✉ **San Michele** 🚣 **Cimitero: Nos 12, 13, 41 & 42** ⊘ Oct-Mar: 7.30am-4pm; Apr-Sept: 7.30am-6pm ⑤ free ♿ limited

Squero di San Trovaso (3, K5)

On the leafy banks of the Rio di San Trovaso, one of Venice's most attractive waterways, you can see one of the few working *squeri* (gondola workshops) left in the city. From the right bank look across to the vessels in various states of (dis)repair.

✉ **Campo San Trovaso, Dorsoduro 1097** 🚣 **Zattere: Nos 51, 52, 61, 62, 82 & N**

Teatro Malibran

(3, C13) They say that this 17th century theatre, which has recently reopened (p. 98), was built over what had been the family abode of Marco Polo. It is claimed that traces of the house were found during the restoration work on the theatre, which ended in 2001.

✉ **Calle del Teatro, San Marco 5870** ☎ **041 78 65 20** ℮ **www.teatrolafenice.it** 🚣 **Rialto: Nos 1, 4, 82 & N** ♿ limited

The Oldest Profession

In the 1530s, Venice had about 11,000 registered prostitutes of a population of 120,000. Attitudes towards the profession changed with each generation, but in the late 15th century a city ordinance stipulated that the ladies of the night should hawk barebreasted. It appears that La Serenissima was concerned that its men were increasingly turning to sodomy. Fearing for Venetian manhood, prostitution was encouraged and sodomy made punishable by death.

A Lopsided Look

Making a good gondola is no easy task – seven different types of wood are employed to make 280 pieces for the hull alone, which *must* be asymmetrical. The left side has a greater curve to make up for the lateral action of the oar, and the cross section is skewed to the right to counterbalance the weight of the gondolier.

Art or a craft? Gondolas painted on a gondola!

Damien Simons

Gondola Rides

Once *the* means of getting around Venice, these strangely shaped vessels remain for many the quintessence of romantic Venice. You can hire them for little tours or even as taxis if you have lots of cash.

✉ **San Marco (☎ 041 520 06 85); Rialto (☎ 041 522 49 04); Piazzale Roma (☎ 041 522 11 51); Stazione di Santa Lucia (☎ 041 71 85 43) ⑤ €62 for 50mins (€77.50 after 8pm) – try to bargain**

KEEPING FIT

Being as tightly packed as the city is, Venice does not make an ideal place to come to practise your favourite sport, whichever one it is that you're passionate about.

Just walking around and up and down bridges means that you're likely to be getting a pretty good workout! A couple of small municipal swimming pools operate (except in summer) along with a handful of small gyms. There is also the opportunity to take up rowing. A couple of jogging options are also suggested below.

Jogging (2, J13)

If you cannot live without a run, the best place to do it is around the Giardini Pubblici and Isola di Sant'Elena. At least here you'll get a little oxygen and not bump into too many people.

✉ **Giardini Pubblici, Castello 🚤 Giardini: Nos 1, 41, 42, 51, 52, 61, 62, 82 & N**

Palestra Body World

(3, B8) Surprising what you can find in the darkest of tiny lanes in Venice. Here is a decent gym with the usual options for cardiovascular exercise and body building. The emphasis

seems to be on the latter however.

✉ **Calle del Ravano, Santa Croce 2196/a ☎ 041 71 56 36 🚤 San Stae: Nos 1 & N ⏰ Sept-May: Mon-Fri 9am-10pm, Sat-Sun 9am-12.30pm; June-Aug: Mon-Fri 9am-10pm ⑤ 1 day €7.75; 1 month €41.35 (plus €25.85 registration)**

Palestra Club Delfino

(2, H6) You could do a little jogging along the Fondamenta Zattere before wandering into this fairly compact health club. Although most people who come are members, if you

need a workout with weights or machines, you can sign for short periods of as little as a day.

✉ **Fondamenta Zattere, Dorsoduro 788/a ☎ 041 523 27 63 e www.palestraclub delfino.com 🚤 Zattere: Nos 51, 52, 61, 62, 82 & N ⏰ Mon-Fri 9am-10pm, Sat 9am-noon ⑤ 1 day €12.40; 1 week €43.90**

Palestra Fitnessmania

(3, A14) Hidden away in a courtyard off one of Venice's classic narrow lanes, this centre has a weights room,

Technogym equipment and runs aerobics sessions. It is really aimed more at long-term (annual) members, but you can take out a monthly membership.
✉ Calle Stella, Cannaregio 5356
☎ 041 522 86 36
🚊 Fondamente Nuove: Nos 12, 13, 41, 42, 51 & 52 ⏲ Mon-Fri 8am-10pm, Sat-Sun 9am-1pm ⑤ 1 month €43.90 (plus €25.85 registration)

Piscina Comunale A Chimisso (2, J3)

This fairly small pool can get crowded, but at least gives you the chance to get in a few laps. The hours are limited and complicated. They usually work in turns of just over an hour and you pay for one of these shifts.
✉ Sacca S Biagio, Giudecca ☎ 041 528 54 30 🚊 Sacca Fisola: Nos 82 & N ⏲ Sept-June: Mon, Tues &

Thurs 10.30-11.15am & 11.15am-noon & 1-2.30pm, Wed 3.45-5pm, Sat 3.45-5pm & 6.30-8pm, Sun 3-4.30pm & 4.30-6pm ⑤ €3.90 per swim

Piscina Comunale di Sant'Alvise (2, B6)

The only other swimming option is at the opposite end of town. The pool is equally small and respect for lanes minimal – the best you can do is struggle up and down as much as splashing kids permit. The hours situation is similar to that at the other pool.
✉ Campo Sant'Alvise, Cannaregio 3161
☎ 041 71 35 67
🚊 Sant'Alvise: Nos 41, 42, 51 & 52 ⏲ mid-Sept-mid-July: Mon, Wed & Fri 1-2.30pm & 9.30-10.15pm, Tues, Thurs & Sat 3-4.15pm, Sat 5.45-7pm, Sun 10-11am & 11am-noon ⑤ €4.15 per swim

Reale Società Canottieri Bucintoro

(3, K12) Back in 1882 the now oldest rowing club in Venice was established by royal concession. Inspired by the English rowing fraternities of Oxbridge, the club went on to furnish Italy with Olympic champions (the entire gold medal team at the 1952 Olympics were members of Bucintoro). Nowadays the club boasts 285 members of all ages, types and sizes. Outsiders are welcome to join up as long- or short-term members, although organisation is a little ad hoc. Even rank beginners can have a go at learning to row, either *voga veneta* (the local standing version) or the classical sit down style known here as *voga inglese* (English rowing).
✉ **Punta della Dogana, Dorsoduro 10**
☎ 041 522 20 55
🄴 www.bucintoro.org
🚊 Salute: No 1

When in Venice, voga veneta *as the Venetians do.*

Damien Simonis

VENICE FOR CHILDREN

Art and architecture might not keep the kids amused for long but there is plenty of interesting activity on the city's waterways. A *gelato* (ice cream) at strategic intervals also often works wonders. You cannot avoid the bridges so leave prams at home and invest in a baby backpack.

I'll wind this one up again.

Damien Simonis

Campanile (3, G13)
See p. 40.

Fondaco dei Turchi (3, A7)
A domineering 19th century facade hides a fine 12th and 13th century building, where in the 17th century the Turkish trading community took up residence. Inside is the **Museo Civico di Storia Naturale** (Natural History Museum), whose displays include a 12m long crocodile that could be one for the kids.
✉ Salizzada del Fondaco dei Turchi, Santa Croce 1730
☎ 041 524 08 85
⚓ traghetto San Marcuola–Salizzada del Fondaco dei Turchi (Mon-Sat 9am-12.30pm); vaporetto Riva de Biasio or San Stae: Nos 1 & N
⊙ opens in 2003

Giardini Pubblici (2, J13) The most extensive public park in Venice is looking a little tatty, but it's better than nothing and you will find swings and things to amuse the little ones. A handy restaurant/bar with outdoor seating completes the picture.
✉ Giardini Pubblici, Castello ⚓ Giardini: Nos 1, 41, 42, 51, 52, 61, 62, 82 & N
♿ limited

Lido Beaches (5, E8)
To escape the summer swelter take the kids to the beach. This involves a soothing ferry ride to the Lido and then either walking to nearby pay beaches or getting a bus or rental bicycles to look for free beaches farther south (such as at Alberoni).
✉ Lido ⚓ Lido: Nos 1, 6, 14, 20, 51, 52, 61, 62, 82 & N ⓢ €10.35-41.35 to rent a chair, umbrella and changing cabin on some beaches
♿ limited

Museo Storico Navale (2, G11)
See p. 39.

Parco Savorgnan (4, D3) You'd hardly know this quiet, well hidden park existed unless directed there. It is a fairly small affair but has a few swings and diversions for the wee bairns and can come as a welcome relief from the chaos in the railway station area.
✉ Fondamenta Savorgnan, Cannaregio
☎ 041 521 70 11
⚓ Guglie: Nos 41, 42, 51 & 52 ⊙ Oct-Mar: 8am-5.30pm; Apr-Sept: 8am-7.30pm ♿ good

Vaporetto No 1
This one really is a must for all the family. Hop aboard the all stops No 1 vaporetto from your arrival point (for most the train station or Piazzale Roma) and chug along the Grand Canal. It's a trip kids aged one to 100 can do time and again without getting bored.
⚓ No 1 ♿ limited

Sitting Babies

If you'd prefer to have a quiet dinner without the little 'uns, or escape for the day, the bigger hotels have child-minding services. Some of the smaller places may be able to help arrange something. If you want to go it alone, some kindergartens *(asili nido)* have lists of babysitters. One option is to contact Codess Sociale, Via Cecchini 45 (☎ 041 534 14 37), a cooperative that usually has lists of available babysitters.

out & about

WALKING TOURS
Rambling to the Rialto

Start by the magnificent facades of the Chiesa dei SS Giovanni e Paolo ❶ and the Scuola Grande di San Marco ❷. Pass below the statue of Bartolomeo Colleoni ❸ as you cross the bridge and head west for the Chiesa di Santa Maria dei Miracoli ❹. From its entrance proceed southeast across the Rio di San Marina and swing westwards – you will see the Teatro Malibran ❺ as you make for the Chiesa di San Giovanni Crisostomo ❻ before turning south past the grim Fondaco dei Tedeschi ❼ for Campo San Bartolomeo ❽. After saluting Goldoni's statue go west for Venice's emblematic bridge, the Ponte di Rialto ❾, which leads to the area of the same name. Once the financial hub of Venice, it is a crush of human activity as people flock to the markets. On your right is the Renaissance Palazzo dei

Damien Simonis

The marvellous marble Ponte di Rialto

Camerlenghi ❿ and just beyond that the Chiesa di San Giacomo di Rialto ⓫. To your left is the Palazzo dei Dieci Savi (Palace of the Ten Wise Men) ⓬. In its shadow stands the Fabbriche Vecchie ⓭. Passing the Fabbriche Nuove ⓮ you finish at the 700 year old Fish Market (Pescaria) ⓯, rebuilt in 1907.

---

distance 1km   **duration** 45mins
▶ **start** 🚉 Ospedale Civile: Nos 41, 42, 51 & 52
● **end** 🚉 Ca' d'Oro: Nos 1 & N

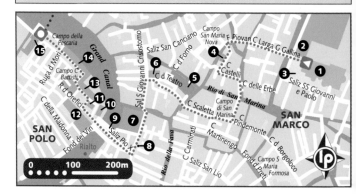

Bridge to Bridge

Start at the apex of the high-arched Ponte dei Scalzi **1** and take in the views over the Grand Canal before crossing into the Sestiere di Santa Croce, where you will pass the grand stone iconostasis that marks the entrance to the Scuola Grande di San Giovanni Evangelista **2**. Cross Campo San Stin and two bridges to reach the impressive Gothic hulk of the Chiesa di Santa Maria Gloriosa dei Frari **3** and, around the corner, the wedding cake facade of Scuola Grande di San Rocco **4**, with its feast

Take an architectural amble.

Damien Simonis

distance 2km	**duration** 1.5hrs
▶ **start**	🚉 Ferrovia: Nos 1, 3, 4, 41, 42, 51, 52, 71, 72, 82 & N
● **end**	🚉 Accademia: Nos 1, 3, 4, 82 & N

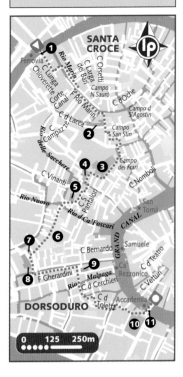

of Tintoretto inside. Continuing south you skirt the Chiesa di San Pantalon **5** en route to the lively Campo Santa Margherita **6**, at the end of which are located the Scuola Grande dei Carmini **7**, with its fine Tiepolos, and the Chiesa dei Carmini **8**. Stop for a *spritz* (p. 95) in the square before crossing the canal to the south and heading east for the Chiesa di San Barnaba **9**. From here follow Calle de Toletta and cross the Rio di Trovaso to arrive at the Gallerie dell'Accademia **10**. Right in front you can climb the Ponte dell'Accademia **11** to enjoy one of Venice's most famous views.

Waterfront Wander

Begin at magnificent St Mark's Square ❶, where you could while away hours contemplating the splendour of St Mark's Basilica, the Doge's Palace, Campanile, Torre dell'Orologio and more. Turn into Piazzetta di San Marco and pass between the statue-symbols of Venice, St Theodore and St Mark (represented by the lion), which front the Bacino di San Marco.

Turn east. On the first bridge look north to the Bridge of Sighs (Ponte dei Sospiri) ❷ and then duck up Calle degli Albanesi for the Museo Diocesano d'Arte Sacra ❸ to admire the Romanesque cloister. Head east along Salizzada San Provolo to reach the Chiesa di San Zaccaria ❹, from whose square you return to the waterfront and again turn eastwards. The lagoonside stroll takes you past Chiesa della Pietà ❺, Vivaldi's church, and on to the Museo Storico Navale ❻ and, nearby, the once mighty shipyards of the Arsenale ❼. Back by

SIGHTS & HIGHLIGHTS

St Mark's Square (p. 30)
Bridge of Sighs (p. 17)
Museo Diocesano d'Arte Sacra (p. 38)
Chiesa di San Zaccaria (p. 45)
Chiesa della Pietà (p. 99)
Museo Storico Navale (p. 39)
Arsenale (p. 40)
Giardini Pubblici (p. 54)
Chiesa di Sant'Elena (p. 49)

Detail of St Mark's Basilica

the water, swing inland along Castello's main drag, Via G Garibaldi, where you plunge into local life, before dropping south through the green space of the Giardini Pubblici ❽ to the peaceful waterfront again. Finally cross the leafy, residential island of Sant'Elena, capped by the city's football stadium, the Stadio Penzo, to the Chiesa di Sant'Elena ❾.

distance 3.4km   **duration** 2hrs
▶ **start** 🚏 Vallaresso, San Marco & San Zaccaria: Nos 1, 3, 4, 6, 14, 41, 42, 51, 52, 71, 72, 82 & N
● **end** 🚏 Sant'Elena: Nos 1, 41, 42, 51, 52, 61 & 62

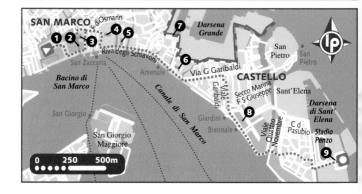

Giudecca the Obscure

Now a working class residential island, Giudecca has been in its time home to patriarchal retreats, the Jewish community and 19th century heavy industry. A stroll here takes you to a little-explored underside of Venice. Start at the Chiesa delle Zitelle ❶. As you head west, duck down Calle Michelangelo and poke around the broad lanes between the low-rise housing blocks. A couple of eateries, kids playing football, washing hung like a forest canopy across the streets – it is a world far from the cramped elegance of Venice. You can occasionally get a glimpse of some of the mansions' impressive private gardens, a luxury enjoyed by a lucky few. Back on the northern esplanade, you pass by Palladio's Chiesa del SS Redentore ❷. As you stroll westwards, enjoy the views of Dorsoduro across the Canale della Giudecca. When you reach the Chiesa di Sant'Eufemia ❸ swing south and you can see how the bell tower of the former Chiesa di SS Cosma e Damiano ❹ was turned into a factory smoke stack! Pursue the way west past the women's prison ❺ to the formidable Molino Stucky ❻, once a factory and destined to be a hotel and apartment complex. Over the bridge and you are in working class Sacca Fisola.

SIGHTS & HIGHLIGHTS

Chiesa delle Zitelle (p. 47)
Chiesa del SS Redentore (p. 47)
Molino Stucky (p. 51)

Damien Simonis

The easily admired SS Redentore

distance 2.5km	**duration** 1hr
▶ **start** 🚏 Zitelle: Nos 41, 42, 82 & N	
● **end** 🚏 Sacca Fisola: Nos 82 & N	

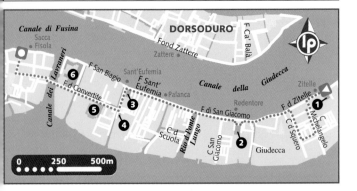

EXCURSIONS

Treviso   (1, B7)

Formerly an important Roman centre, Treviso has a pleasant medieval centre and is well worth a day's exploration.

Piazza dei Signori is dominated by the fine brick **Palazzo dei Trecento**, the one time seat of city government. You can now stop for coffee and a bite to eat beneath the vaults. The medieval main street is porticoed Via Calmaggiore, which leads to the **cathedral** *(duomo)*, Piazza del Duomo (Mon-Fri 7.30am-noon & 3.30-7pm, Sat-Sun 7.30am-1pm & 3.30-8pm), a massive structure whose main interest lies in the frescoes by Il Pordenone.

Meander around behind the Palazzo dei Trecento and you'll find yourself in a warren of lanes that leads to five delightful bridges across the leafy Canal Cagnan, which runs roughly north-south and spills into the River Sile at a particularly pleasant corner where parts of the city wall remain intact. You will see the occasional mill wheel (the one by Vicolo Molinetto still turns). Pop into the deconsecrated **Chiesa di Santa Caterina**, Via di Santa Caterina (1st Sun of month 9am-noon & 3-7pm; €1.55), decorated with frescoes by Tommaso da Modena. Tommaso also left frescoes in the imposing **Chiesa di San Nicolò**, Via San Nicolò (7am-noon & 3.30-7pm), on the other side of town.

Treviso claims Luciano Benetton, the clothing manufacturer, as its favourite son – they have a big store, Piazza dell'Indipendenza 5 (☎ 0422 55 99 11; Mon 3.30-7.30pm, Tues-Sat 10am-7.30pm) in the heart of town.

Damien Simonis

Fine-feathered Italians out for a stroll

Padua   (1, C5)

A medieval university town, Padua is surprisingly rich in art treasures, and its many piazzas and arcaded streets are a pleasure to explore. Before coming under Venice's sway, Padua reached the height of its glory under the counts of Carrara in the 13th century.

Giotto's remarkable fresco cycle in the **Cappella degli Scrovegni**, Giardini dell'Arena (obligatory bookings ☎ 049 820 45 50; closed for restoration; €5.20 plus €1.05 booking fee) was completed by 1306 and presages the creative explosion of the Renaissance. Admission is valid for the adjacent **Museo Civico** (Tues-Sun 9am-7pm), which contains a notable crucifix by Giotto.

The nucleus of old Padua is formed by Piazza delle Erbe and Piazza della Frutta, which are separated by the majestic **Palazzo della Ragione** (Mar-Oct: Tues-Sun 9am-7pm; Nov-Feb: Tues-Sun 9am-6pm; €5.20 depending on exhibitions). The building boasts fine frescoes. The **cathedral**, Piazza del Duomo (Mon-Sat 7.30am-noon & 3.45-7pm, Sun & hols 7.45am-1pm & 3.45-8.30pm) was built to a much altered design by

INFORMATION

37km west of Venice

- 🚋 Padua; up to 40mins
- ⓘ tourist office, Vicolo Pedrocchi (☎ 049 876 79 27), and at the train station
- Ⓢ Padova Arte (€7.75/5.20) for all main sights
- ✕ Per Bacco, Piazzale Pontecorvo 10 (☎ 049 802 23 27)

Relax alfresco between explorations.

Damien Simonis

Horsing Around

The sculptor Donatello raised the equestrian statue of the Venetian mercenary Erasmos da Narni, known as *Gattamelata* (Honeyed Cat), in Piazza del Santo. He made a lasting impression on Padua, leaving behind a whole school of sculptors that followed in his footsteps. They would come to specialise in bronze miniatures *(bronzetti)*, coveted across Europe.

Michelangelo and has a 13th century Romanesque **baptistry** (10am-6pm; €2.10).

Pilgrims flock to the **Basilica del Santo** (or di Sant'Antonio), Piazza del Santo (6.30am-7.30pm), which houses the tomb and relics of the town's patron saint (St Anthony).

Vicenza   (1, B4)

Vicenza flourished as Roman Vicentia and in 1404 was incorporated into the Venetian Republic. Palladio's work is today the main attraction.

Piazza dei Signori is dominated by the immense **Basilica Palladiana** (☎ 0444 32 36 81; Tues-Sun 9am-5pm), on which Palladio started work in 1549 over an earlier Gothic building (whose 12th century bell tower remains).

Contrà Porti is one of the city's most majestic streets. The **Palazzo Thiene** at No 12, by Lorenzo da Bologna, was originally intended to occupy the entire block. Palladio's richly decorated **Palazzo Barbaran da Porto** (☎ 0444 32 30 14; Tues-Sun 10am-6pm; €5.20) at No 11 features a double row of columns, and frequently hosts exhibitions. Palladio also built the unfinished **Palazzo Isoppo da Porto** at No 21.

Palladio and Vincenzo Scamozzi designed the **Teatro Olimpico**, Corso Andrea Palladio (☎ 0444 22 28 00; Sept-June: Tues-Sun 9am-5pm; Jul-Aug: Tues-Sun 10am-7pm; €6.75), which is considered to be one of the purest creations of Renaissance architecture.

A little tired after all those years?

South of the centre, the 18th century hill-top **Basilica di Monte Bèrico**, Piazzale della Vittoria (Mon-Sat 6.15am-12.30pm & 2.30-7.30pm, Sun & hols 6.15am-8pm) presents magnificent views.

A 20 minute walk along Viale X Giugno and east along Via San Bastiano takes you to the **Villa Valmarana 'ai Nani'**. From there a path leads to Palladio's Villa Capra, which is better known as **La Rotonda** (☎ 0444 32 17 93; Mar-Nov: Wed 10am-noon & 3-6pm; €5.20). It is one of the architect's most admired – and copied – creations, having served as a model for buildings across Europe and the USA.

Renaissance shell of the Basilica Palladiana

Verona   (1, C1)

Known as 'little Rome', Verona came into its own during the 13th and 14th centuries under the della Scala family (aka the Scaligeri). The period was noted for savage family feuding to which Shakespeare alluded in *Romeo and Juliet*. The city is one of the most attractive in northern Italy.

The pink marble **Roman Arena**, Piazza Brà (☎ 045 800 32 04; Tues-Sun 9am-6.30pm, during opera seasons 8am-3.30pm; €3.10), built in the 1st century AD, is the third largest Roman amphitheatre in existence and does a roaring trade as Verona's opera house.

Romantics head for **Juliet's House** (Casa di Giulietta), Via Cappello 23 (☎ 045 803 43 03; Tues-Sat 9am-6.30pm; €3.10). You can swoon beneath what popular myth says was her balcony or, if in need of a new lover, approach a bronze statue of Juliet and rub her right breast for good luck.

Originally the site of a Roman forum, **Piazza delle Erbe** remains the lively heart of the city today. It is lined with sumptuous buildings, including the Baroque **Palazzo Maffei**, at the northern end, with the adjoining 14th century **Torre**

Verona's ancient and expansive Arena

Damien Simonis

del Gardello. On the eastern side is the frescoed **Casa Mazzanti**, a former della Scala family residence. Ascend the nearby 12th century **Torre dei Lamberti** (Tues-Sun 9am-6pm; by elevator €2.10, on foot €1.55) for a great view of the city.

The 15th century **Loggia del Consiglio**, the former city council building at the northern end of Piazza dei Signori, is regarded as Verona's finest Renaissance structure. It is attached to the **Palazzo degli Scaligeri**, once the main residence of the della Scala family. The tombs of the **Arche Scaligere**, Piazza dei Signori (Tues-Sun 9am-6pm; with Torre dei Lamberti €2.60) are an elaborate memorial to the della Scala family.

Verona is blessed with some fine churches (combined ticket €4.15, admission to each €2.10). Among the most interesting is the 12th century **cathedral**, Piazza del Duomo (Mon-Sat 10am-5.30pm, Sun 1.30-5.30pm), which combines Romanesque (lower section) and Gothic (upper section) styles and has some intriguing features. Look for the sculpture of Jonah and the Whale on the southern porch and the statues of two of Charlemagne's paladins, Roland and Oliver, on the western porch. In the first chapel of the left aisle is an *Assumption* by Titian, in an altar frame by Jacopo Sansovino. The Gothic **Chiesa di Sant'Anastasia**, Piazza di Sant'Anastasia (Mon-Sat 9am-6pm, Sun 1-6pm), started in 1290 but not completed until the late 15th century, contains numerous artworks including a fresco by Pisanello depicting St George freeing a princess from the dragon.

An attractive corner of 'little Rome'

Chiesa di San Fermo, Stradone San Fermo (Mon-Sat 10am-6pm, Sun 1-6pm), is actually two: the Gothic church was built in the 13th century over the original 11th century Romanesque structure. The **Chiesa di San Lorenzo**, Corso Cavour (Mon-Sat 10am-6pm, Sun 1-6pm) is near the Castelvecchio and the **Basilica di San Zeno Maggiore**, Piazza San Zeno 2 (Mon-Sat 8.30am-6pm, Sun 1-6pm), a masterpiece of Romanesque architecture, farther west. The latter was built mainly in the 12th century and the magnificent rose window depicts the Wheel of Fortune. The highlight inside is Andrea Mantegna's triptych of the Virgin and Child.

On the banks of the Adige, the 14th century **Castelvecchio** fortress, Corso Castelvecchio 2 (☎ 045 59 47 34; Tues-Sun 9am-6.30pm; €3.10) houses a museum with a diverse collection including works by Giovanni Bellini, Tiepolo, Carpaccio and Veronese.

Across Ponte Pietra is a **Roman theatre**, built in the 1st century AD and still used for concerts and plays.

The gladiators have gone but you can catch an open-air opera at the amphitheatre.

Villa Foscari (La Malcontenta)(5, D1)

Past the nightmare industryscape of Marghera lies the peaceful retreat of Villa Foscari. Here, the Foscari family commissioned Palladio to construct a pleasure dome on the River Brenta. The result was a Palladian trademark: the riverside facade with its ionic columns and classical tympanum, echoing the ancients that inspired him. It is also known as La Malcontenta (the malcontent), supposedly because a female family member was exiled here for fooling around with people other than her hubby. Its interior is remarkable only for the frescoes with which it is covered.

Soak up the atmosphere at La Malcontenta.

Bassano del Grappa (1, A4)

Known for its firewater, grappa, Bassano del Grappa sits astride the River Brenta within sight of the Dolomites. The centre is composed of two interlinking squares, Piazza Garibaldi and Piazza Libertà, watched over by the remains of the medieval **Castello Ezzelini**.

The **Museo Civico**, Via del Museo 12 (☎ 0424 52 22 35; Tues-Sat 9am-6pm, Sun 3.30-6.30pm; €2.60) contains archaeological finds and Renaissance art.

The **Ponte degli Alpini** is named after Alpine troops who rebuilt it in 1948. The **Poli Museo della Grappa**, Ponte Vecchio (☎ 0424 52 44 26; 9am-1pm & 2.30-7.30pm; free) is in the Poli grappa shop.

Villas on the Stream

Dotted along the River Brenta are more than 100 villas built over the centuries by wealthy Venetian families. Usually some are open to the public (mostly Apr-Sept only) and you can reach them on the bus to Padua. Several companies also run villa cruises between Venice and Strà (1, C6). Il Burchiello (☎ 049 877 47 12, Ⓔ www.ilburchiello.it) is the main one. Ask for details at the Venice (p. 114) or Padua (p. 60) tourist offices.

ORGANISED TOURS

Travel agents all over Venice can organise tours of the city, islands and villas of the River Brenta. *Un Ospite di Venezia* (p. 92) details other visits to churches and sights in the city. The APT office has a list of authorised walking-tour guides. Many museums such as the Doge's Palace (p. 16) can also organise guided tours at a price. The Museo Archeologico (p. 26) and Libreria Nazionale Marciana (p. 26) also offer free tours.

Città d'Acqua (Cities on Water) (5, A2)

The Maree Veneziane tours explore various parts of the lagoon, including the Arsenale (otherwise virtually impossible to visit), Malamocco, Le Vignole and Giudecca, with an emphasis on environmental problems and aspects of preserving Venice against flood waters.

☒ **Centro Internazionale Città d'Acqua, Officina Viaggi, Mestre**
☎ **041 523 04 28**
e **www.venice itineraries.com**
◷ **variable (minimum 10-40 people required)**
⑤ **up to €70 per person (minimum group of 40), up to €90 per person (group of 10-39)**

Codessa Cultura

This outfit runs guided visits of the Jewish cemetery on the Lido. See p. 24.

Delta Tour (1, C5)

The Padua-based Delta Tour company offers a series of full-day boat tours, one of Venice and the main lagoon islands (Murano, Burano and Torcello), another of the Brenta Riviera villas and a third of the River Po delta.

☒ **Via Toscana 2/a, Padua** ☎ **049 870 02 32** ◷ **Apr-Oct when sufficient numbers allow** ⑤ **€41-57**

Gita Alle Isole

This is an unguided trip by boat to the three main islands of interest in the lagoon, Burano (p. 15), Murano (p. 25) and Torcello (p. 36). The main benefit of the tour is that you don't have to wait around for ferries, although for some that can be part of the fun.

☒ **Serenissima Motoscafi, Castello 4545** ☎ **041 522 42 81**
◷ **9.30am, 3½hrs**
⑤ **€15.50**

Jewels of the Venetian Republic (3, H11)

The grand sounding name of the tour should not blind you to the fact that it is basically a jaunt around St Mark's Square, with inspections of St Mark's Basilica and the Palazzo Ducale. You can request a glass-blowing demonstration too.

☒ **American Express, Salizzada San Moisè, San Marco 1471** ☎ **041 520 08 44** ◷ **(English) 9.10am, 2hrs** ⑤ **€25**

Magic & Enchantment of Venetian Life

(3, H11) You are guided through the streets of the Sestiere di San Marco and then across the Grand Canal by gondola to visit the Frari (p. 33). It's then on to the Rialto by gondola along back canals.

☒ **American Express, Salizzada San Moisè, San Marco 1471**
☎ **041 520 08 44**
◷ **(English) Apr-Oct 3pm, 2½hrs** ⑤ **€28.50**

St Mark's Mosaics

(3, G13) The Patriarcato (church body in Venice) organises guided tours of the mosaics in St Mark's Basilica. You are given a detailed explanation of their biblical significance. The timetable can vary so call ahead to be sure.

☒ **Piazza San Marco, San Marco** ☎ **041 270 24 21** ◷ **(English) Mon, Thurs, Fri 11am; (French) Thurs 11am; (Italian) Mon-Tues & Thurs-Sat 11am** ⑤ **free**

I Want to be Alone!

My Venice hand-held itinerary earpieces, available at the Venice Pavilion tourist office (3, J12), allow you to follow commented itineraries to key parts of the city for anything from an hour (€3.65) to two days (€15.50). Languages catered for are Italian, English, French and German. You need to leave your passport as a deposit.

shopping

There is no shortage of shops in which to make your plastic bleed. If classic Venetian items such as Murano glass, lace, marbled paper and Carnevale masks don't do it for you, a host of other options, from high Italian fashion to curious handicrafts, will entice you.

Tax Refunds

A value added tax of around 19%, known as IVA, is slapped onto just about everything in Italy. If you are resident outside the EU and spend more than €155 in the same shop on the same day, you can claim a refund on this tax when you leave the EU. The refund only applies to purchases from affiliated retail outlets that display a 'Tax free for Tourists' sign. You have to complete a form at the point of sale, then get it stamped by Italian customs as you leave. At major airports you can get an immediate cash refund.

Shopping Areas

The main shopping area for clothing, shoes, accessories and jewellery is in the narrow streets between St Mark's Square (3, G13) and the Rialto (3, D11), particularly the Mercerie and around Campo San Luca (3, F11). The more upmarket shops are west of St Mark's Square.

For Carnevale masks, costumes, ceramics and model gondolas, **San Polo** (3) is the best place to hunt. Another Venetian speciality, marbled paper, is found all over town. **Murano** glass can be obtained on the island (5, C7) or in shops mainly in the Sestiere di San Marco. Lace, another speciality, is most easily bought on the island of **Burano** (5, B9), although several shops in Venice also sell it.

Opening Hours

Store opening hours are about 9.30am to 7.30pm, with a two hour break from around 1pm. Bigger stores and increasingly some small shops skip the lunch break. Treat the hours given in this chapter with caution – often the final arbiter is the whim of the shop owner. Most shops open Saturday and some, anxious to attract every tourist euro, on Sunday too. Several shops shut through at least part of August.

Artistic anonymity: the Venetian way to party with impunity

Damien Simonis

ART

The single biggest concentration of galleries, selling a variety of art, is on the streets that lie between the Gallerie dell'Accademia (3, K6) and the Peggy Guggenheim Collection (3, K8). A few stragglers line Calle del Bastion (3, K9). Another area that might be worth a look is Calle delle Carrozze (3, G6), in San Marco.

GALLERIES

Bugno Samueli Art Gallery (3, H10)
This luxury gallery has some works by contemporary artists on permanent display, although sales are the primary objective. While you might not be able to afford a Mirò or de Chirico, there's plenty of other material for the modern art collector.
⊠ Campo San Fantin, San Marco 1996/a ☎ 041 523 13 05 🛴 Santa Maria del Giglio: No 1 ⏲ Tues-Sat 10.30am-12.30pm & 4-7.30pm, Sun-Mon 4-7.30pm

Galleria Traghetto
(3, H9) In this rather limited space you can usually inspect a sample of modern painting and sculpture. Some works are by local artists. The gallery gives a particularly strong run to Fabrizio Plessi, whose catalogues adorn the place.
⊠ Calle del Piovan, San Marco 2543 ☎ 041 522 11 88 🛴 Santa Maria del Giglio: No 1 ⏲ Mon-Sat 10.30am-12.30pm & 3.30-7.30pm

Studio Aoristico di Matteo lo Greco
(3, H10) Matteo lo Greco runs a curious one man show of his own contemporary sculpture and paintings in this tiny studio space near what is left of

La Fenice theatre.
⊠ Campo San Fantin, San Marco 1998 ☎ 041 521 25 82 🛴 Santa Maria del Giglio: No 1 ⏲ Mon-Sat 11am-1pm & 4-8pm, Sun 4-8pm

PRINTS

BAC Art Studio (3, K7)
This studio has paintings, aquatints and engravings by Cadore and Paolo Baruffaldi that can make fine gifts. They are a cut above the pictures of Venice available at street stalls (and a little pricier too). Cadore concentrates his commercial efforts on street and canal scenes, while Baruffaldi depicts masked people. There are also quality postcards.
⊠ Campo San Vio, Dorsoduro 862 ☎ 041 522 81 71 🛴 Accademia: Nos 1, 3, 4, 82 & N ⏲ Mon-Sat 10am-1pm & 3-7pm

Galleria Ferruzzi
(3, K8) Ferruzzi's images of Venice are an engaging, almost naïve distortion of what we see. With fat brush strokes and primary colours, the artist creates a kind of children's gingerbread Venice. You'll find screen prints, paintings and even postcard versions on sale here.
⊠ Fondamenta Zorzi Bragadin, Dorsoduro 523 ☎ 041 520 59 96 🛴 Accademia: Nos 1,

3, 4, 82 & N ⏲ 10am-6.30pm

La Stamperia del Ghetto (4, B5)
The ghetto houses a huddle of interesting little shops. At the Stamperia you can pick up prints of old Venice and other images more closely associated with the Ghetto itself.
⊠ Calle del Ghetto Vecchio, Cannaregio 1185/a ☎ 041 275 02 00 🛴 Guglie: Nos 41, 42, 51 & 52 ⏲ Sun-Fri 10am-5pm

Schola San Zaccaria
(3, H8) Another variation on the prints theme is this intriguing place, where you will find only works depicting characters of the Commedia dell'Arte, such as Arlecchino (Harlequin). The movement and colour in some of the paintings and prints make them stand out from much of the standard Venetian print fare.
⊠ Campo San Maurizio, San Marco 2664 ☎ 041 523 43 43 🛴 Santa Maria del Giglio: No 1 ⏲ Sun-Fri 10am-1pm & 2-6.45pm

SUPPLIES

Artemisia (3, E6)
In this well stocked arts supplies shop you can get just about anything imaginable for painting, restoration, sculpture and so on. It's perfect for the artist inspired by

the lagoon city. Students get 20% off.
✉ **Campiello Zen, San Polo 972** ☎ 041 244 02 90 🚣 San Tomà: Nos 1, 82 & N ⏰ Mon 3-7pm, Tues-Sun 9.30am-12.30pm & 3-7pm

Cartoleria Accademia (3, G3) This store has been selling artists' supplies since 1810. The place looks a little as if

there haven't been any renovations since it first opened, but it does have a decent range of materials on offer.
✉ **Campo Santa Margherita, Dorsoduro 2928** ☎ 041 520 70 86 🚣 Ca' Rezzonico: No 1 ⏰ Mon-Sat 10am-7pm

Testolini (3, G11)
Art supplies seem to be the main line of work in this curious shop, but if

you are feeling nautical you may want to drop in as well: in one section you will find an odd collection of model sailing ships, ships in bottles and other seafaring objects.
✉ **Fondamenta Orseolo, San Marco 1756** ☎ 041 277 08 12 🚣 Vallaresso & San Marco: Nos 1, 3, 4, 82 & N ⏰ Mon-Sat 9am-1pm & 3-7pm; Sun 11am-6pm

ANTIQUES & CRAFTS

In Venice you can track down all sorts of antiques and interesting crafts, from crazy, wooden raincoats (no help in the rain at all!) to model gondolas.

A Mano (3, D6)
This shop is full of all sorts of decorative items and all goods are handmade. Quirky lampshades, mirrors and a host of other gewgaws certainly make it an interesting stop for some window shopping.
✉ **Rio Terrà, San Polo 2616** ☎ 041 71 57 42 🚣 San Tomà: Nos 1, 82 & N ⏰ Mon-Sat 10am-1.30pm & 2.30-7.30pm

Antiquus (3, G7)
This inviting little shop boasts a solid collection of old masters, silverware and antique jewellery. Alongside the few items of furniture sit grand tea sets and other aristo bric-a-brac.
✉ **Calle delle Botteghe, San Marco 3131** ☎ 041 520 63 95 🚣 San Samuele: Nos 1, 3, 4, 82 & N ⏰ Mon 3.30-7.30pm, Tues-Sun 10am-12.30pm & 3.30-7.30pm

Cenerentola (3, E6)
Every conceivable kind of lampshade is on display,

although the tendency is towards classic pieces, often made of old embroidered cloth with a 19th century feel – nothing slick and modern here. You can buy shades ready made or have one created to order. They also purvey antique lace.
✉ **Calle dei Saoneri, San Polo 2718** ☎ 041 527 44 55 🚣 San Tomà: Nos 1, 82 & N ⏰ Mon 10.30am-1pm, Tues-Sun 10.30am-1pm & 2.30-8pm

Gilberto Penzo (3, E6)
Here you can buy exquisite hand-built wooden models of various Venetian vessels. Mr Penzo also takes in old ones for restoration. For the kids, you can fork out about €25 on gondola model kits (or buy them ready made and painted). Poster-size technical drawings of Venice's floating symbol sell for around €10. And round the corner, you can have a peek at Penzo's workshop.
✉ **Calle Saoneri, San**

Polo 2681 ☎ 041 71 93 72 🚣 San Tomà: Nos 1, 82 & N ⏰ Mon-Sat 9.30am-12.30pm & 3-6pm

Jesurum (3, E12)
Jesurum has been in business since 1860, when Michelangelo Jesurum opened a lace school on the Burano island, then a deeply poor backwater. The quality and complexity of the women's work was such that Jesurum's laces won a prize at the 1878 Universal Exposition. Since then, Burano lace has come to be known worldwide and Jesurum remains *the* name to look for.
✉ **Merceria del Capitello, San Marco 4856** ☎ 041 520 60 85 🚣 Rialto: Nos 1, 4, 82 & N ⏰ Mon-Sat 9.30am-7.30pm, Sun 10am-1pm & 2-7pm

Kleine Gallery (3, G7)
Another in the Calle delle Botteghe series of antique shops, the Kleine Gallery deals in two main lines.

Among old books and prints, some fine pieces of porcelain and majolica can turn up.

✉ Calle delle Botteghe, San Marco 2972 ☎ 041 522 21 77 🚹 San Samuele: Nos 1, 3, 4, 82 & N ⏰ Mon 4-7.45pm, Tues-Sat 10am-12.45pm & 4-7.45pm

Laboratorio del Gerva (2, G10)

In this higgledy-piggledy workshop are stacked enough goods to whet the appetite of any antiques collector, but if you are a serious purchaser ask to see the warehouse. Michele Gervasuti is continuing the work of his father, Eugenio, a master craftsman who opened the shop in 1959. They concentrate on restoration and are involved in projects across the city.

✉ Campo Bandiera e Moro, Castello 3725 ☎ 041 523 67 77 🚹 San Zaccaria: Nos 1, 6, 14, 41, 42, 51, 52, 71, 72, 82 & N ⏰ 10am-7.30pm

Lapo de' Bardi (3, G7)

We are assured the marquetry creations in this workshop give rise to 'wooden emotions'. Certainly the ingeniousness of the woodwork, used to produce 'paintings' and table tops with equal mastery, is impressive. Virtually no image or series of geometrical shapes is beyond the craftsmanship of de' Bardi.

✉ Salizzada San Samuele, San Marco 3151 ☎ 041 244 74 54 🚹 San Samuele: Nos 1, 3, 4, 82 & N ⏰ Mon-Fri 10.30am-noon & 3.30-7pm

Livio de Marchi

(3, G7) This place, with wooden sculptures of underpants, socks and shirts, is rather strange but endearing all the same. Just what you might do with a fine carving of an unironed shirt in your living room is perhaps a little hard to imagine.

✉ Salizzada San Samuele, San Marco 3157/a ☎ 041 528 56 94 🚹 San Samuele: Nos 1, 3, 4, 82 & N ⏰ Mon-Fri 9am-noon & 2-6pm

Testolini (3, G11)

See p. 68.

Valese (3, F12)

Since 1918 the Valese family have been casting figures in bronze, copper and other metals. Their reputation is unequalled in the city. Not all the items might suggest themselves as souvenirs, but the horses that adorn the flanks of the city's gondolas are tempting.

✉ Calle Fiubera, San Marco 793 ☎ 041 522 72 82 🚹 Vallaresso & San Marco: Nos 1, 3, 4, 82 & N ⏰ Mon 3-7pm, Tues-Sat 10.30am-12.30pm & 3-7pm

Gilberto's Gondolas

Gilberto Penzo long ago became passionate about gondolas. He began to build models and collect detailed plans of them and all other lagoon and Adriatic vessels. He founded an association aimed at keeping all this ancient knowledge fresh, and to finance it all he opened a shop (see p. 68).

Keeping the ancient art afloat at Gilberto Penzo.

Damien Simonis

BOOKS & MUSIC

There are several good book shops in Venice, but English-language titles can be pricey compared with the UK and USA.

Editore Filippi (3, E14)
Don't let the unremarkable appearance fool you. This is a den of books on all manner of subjects related to Venice, many published and only on sale here. The Filippis have been in the book business for nearly a century. Scholars search them out for their tomes and encyclopedic knowledge.
✉ **Calle Casselleria, Castello 5763** ☎ **041 523 56 35** 🚣 San Zaccaria: Nos 1, 6, 14, 41, 42, 51, 52, 71, 72, 82 & N ⏲ Mon-Sat 9am-12.30pm & 3-7.30pm

Libreria al Ponte
(3, F10) This small but useful shop offers a solid range of guides and other books on Venice, as well as children's books, many in English. They stock a good assortment of Donna Leon's mystery detective yarns, all set in Venice.
✉ **Calle della Cortesia, San Marco 3717/d** ☎ **041 522 40 30** 🚣 Rialto: Nos 1, 4, 82 & N ⏲ Mon-Sat 9.30am-9.15pm

Libraire Française
(2, E10) *Voulez-vous vos livres en français?* Here you will find everything from the latest bestsellers of Gallic literature to a plethora of titles on all subjects Venetian – all of it in French.
✉ **Barbaria de le Tole, Castello 6358** ☎ **041 522 96 59** 🚣 Ospedale Civile: Nos 41, 42, 51 & 52 ⏲ Mon 3.30-7pm, Tues-Sat 9am-12.30pm & 3.30-7pm

Libreria Goldoni
(3, E11) One of the city's establishment book shops, this place has an impressive range of material on Venice in Italian, English and French, as well as a broad selection of books covering most subjects in Italian.
✉ **Calle dei Fabbri, San Marco 4742** ☎ **041 522 23 84** 🚣 Rialto: Nos 1, 4, 82 & N ⏲ Mon-Sat 9am-7.30pm

Nalesso (3, H8)
In a small courtyard off the street, Nalesso specialises in music connected with Venice, especially classical, Renaissance, Baroque and opera. If you have revived your interest in Vivaldi or the likes, this is the place to stock up on CDs.
✉ **Calle del Spezier, San Marco 2765/d** ☎ **041 520 33 29** 🚣 Santa Maria del Giglio: No 1 ⏲ Mon-Sat 10am-1pm & 3-7pm

Peggy Guggenheim Museum Shop (3, K8)
Located in the same building as the gallery of the same name (but with a different entrance), the shop offers a select array of coffee-table books and souvenirs related to the gallery's modern-art collections.
✉ **Fondamenta Venier dai Leoni, Dorsoduro 710** ☎ **041 240 54 24** 🚣 Accademia: Nos 1, 3, 4, 82 & N ⏲ Wed-Mon 10am-6pm

San Marco Studium
(3, F14) Just off St Mark's Square, this shop, with books piled high and wide, stocks a broad offering of English-language guides and books on Venice. They have material in other languages too.
✉ **Calle de la Canonica, San Marco 337/a** ☎ **041 522 23 82** 🚣 San Zaccaria: Nos 1, 6, 14, 41, 42, 51, 52, 71, 72, 82 & N ⏲ Mon-Sat 9am-7.30pm

Reading on Venice

- *Art and Life in Renaissance Venice* – Patricia Fortini Brown
- *Across the River and into the Trees* – Ernest Hemingway
- *Venice: the Biography of a City* – Christopher Hibbert
- *A Sea of Troubles* – Donna Leon
- *Death in Venice* – Thomas Mann
- *The Comfort of Strangers* – Ian McEwan
- *Venice* – James (Jan) Morris
- *A History of Venice* – John Julius Norwich
- *The Stones of Venice* – John Ruskin
- *The Merchant of Venice* – William Shakespeare

CARNEVALE MASKS & COSTUMES

Carnevale masks make beautiful souvenirs. Quality and price vary. You can find people selling masks on just about every canal corner, but for serious craftsmanship you have to look a little closer. The cheap touristy rubbish is manufactured industrially (in Padua, for instance) and is worthless. The ceramic masks have absolutely nothing to do with the genuine article, which are carefully crafted objects in papier-mache *(cartapesta)* or leather.

Mask madness!

Atelier Pietro Longhi (3, E6) If you've ever fancied buying a helmet and sword to go with your tailor-made Carnevale costume – or indeed just about any kind of costume item from a Harlequin outfit to 18th century gala wear – this is your shop. Or maybe just buy yourself a top hat?
✉ **Rio Terrà, San Polo 2604/b** ☎ **041 71 44 78** 🚤 **San Tomà: Nos 1, 82 & N** ⏲ Mon-Sat 10am-1pm & 2.30-7.30pm

Ca' del Sole (2, G10) Although much of what is on sale here, especially in terms of costumes, is aimed at the theatre business, anyone can purchase a fantasy in this 'House of the Sun'. The masks are of a high standard.
✉ **Fondamenta dell'Osmarin 4964** ☎ **041 528 55 49** 🚤 **San Zaccaria: Nos 1, 6, 14, 20, 41, 42, 51, 52, 71, 72, 82 & N** ⏲ **10am-8pm**

Ca' Macana (3, H4) Wander in and watch the artists at work on the raw papier-mache of future masks. Apparently Stanley Kubrick was impressed – he made a large order for his last film, *Eyes Wide Shut*. Along black walls the finished products gaze down at you.
✉ **Calle delle Botteghe, Dorsoduro 5176** ☎ **041 520 32 29** 🚤 **Ca' Rezzonico: No 1** ⏲ **Mon-Sat 9.45am-7.45pm, Sun 10am-8pm**

L'Arlecchino (3, C9) Here they claim the masks are made only with papier-mache to their own designs. To prove it you can inspect their workshop and see production from the earliest phases to the finishing touches. The quality of masks is evident. You'll find another **L'Arlecchino** at Ruga del Ravano, San Polo 789 (3, D10).
✉ **Calle dei Cristi, San Polo 1722-1729** ☎ **041 71 65 91** 🚤 **San Silvestro: No 1** ⏲ **9.30am-7.30pm**

Tragicomica (3, E6) One of the city's bigger mask and costume merchants, Tragicomica also organises costume parties during Carnevale. The place is quite overwhelming at first sight.
✉ **Calle Nomboli, San Polo 2800** ☎ **041 72 11 02** 🚤 **San Tomà: Nos 1, 82 & N** ⏲ **10am-1.30pm & 2.30-7pm**

A cornucopia of Carnevalia

CERAMICS

Although Venice does not have a great tradition of ceramics production, many artists have set up shop here and produce a surprising range of material, from classical Sicilian to cheerfully enamelled clocks.

Arca (3, B7)
The designs in this eye-catching shop are powerful, and for some tastes the colours are possibly a little strong. Teresa della Valentina paints her tiles and other ceramic objects in bold, bright, deep colours.
✉ **Calle del Tintor, Santa Croce 1811**
☎ **041 71 04 27**
🚊 **San Stae: Nos 1 & N** ⏰ **9.30am-7.30pm**

Ceramichevolmente (3, G8) Bringing a splash of southern Mediterranean light to the muted northern stage of Venice, Agata d'Alessandro's traditional Sicilian ceramics, ranging from plates to jars and anything in between, show off the limpid blues, yellows and greens that mark her island's long tradition

of ceramic production.
✉ **Calle delle Botteghe, Santa Marco 3455**
☎ **041 522 99 43**
🚊 **Accademia: Nos 1, 3, 4, 82 & N** ⏰ **Mon 3.30-7.30pm, Tues-Sun 10.30am-7.30pm**

La Bottega del Vasaio (3, G3)
Pierluigi Volpini creates some charming pieces in his little workshop here, ranging from plates to coffee containers. The dominant colours are the fairly traditional yellows and blues of mainstream Mediterranean ceramics and make nice additions to the kitchen.
✉ **Campo Santa Margherita, Dorsoduro 2904**
☎ **041 538 73 18**
🚊 **Ca' Rezzonico: No 1** ⏰ **10am-1pm & 2.30-7pm**

La Margherita Ceramiche (3, C8)
The contrast between this place and Arca (see left) couldn't be greater. Margherita Rossetto's kitchen pots, clocks and other hand-painted items are all tranquil designs in soft blues and yellows – an altogether sunnier look.
✉ **Sotoportego de Siora Bettina, Santa Croce 2345** ☎ **041 72 31 20**
🚊 **San Stae: Nos 1 & N** ⏰ **9.30am-7.30pm**

La Margherita Ceramiche

CLOTHING & FABRICS

For a selection of the big-name fashion outlets in Venice, see Fashionable Retail Therapy (p. 73). You will also find the occasional alternative clothing store.

Colorcasa (3, E8)
All sorts of household fabrics, from cushion covers to tablecloths, curtains, sheets and the like, are complemented by clothing items such as scarves, ties and bags in various materials.
✉ **Campo San Polo, San Polo 1989-1991**
☎ **041 523 60 71**
🚊 **San Silvestro: No 1** ⏰ **Mon-Sat 9am-1pm & 3-6.30pm**

Sumptuous Colorcasa

Fiorella Gallery (3, H8) You'll find all sorts of odd billowing and fantastical clothing items here. They adorn transsexual *doge* mannequins scattered about the inside and in the windows of this unique store. It may not be high fashion but it is definitely a source of curiosity.
✉ **Campo Santo Stefano, San Marco**

2806 ☎ 041 520 92 28 🚤 Accademia: Nos 1, 3, 4, 82 & N ⊙ Mon-Sat 10am-7pm

Laboratorio Arte & Costume (3, C7)
What a hodgepodge there is in here! You can get hold of costumes, masks and sometimes rather tacky jewellery. And what about a Father Christmas suit? An oddly eclectic collection of second-hand hats also awaits.
✉ Calle del Scaleter, San Polo 2235
☎ 041 524 62 42 🚤 San Silvestro: No 1 ⊙ 10am-12.30pm & 3-6.30pm

Rubelli (3, G12)
If you are in need of the most luxurious materials for decorating the palace, then come to this emporium and have a look at the exquisite damasks and jacquard.
✉ Campo San Gallo, San Marco 1089
☎ 041 521 64 11 🚤 Vallaresso & San Marco: Nos 1, 3, 4, 82 & N ⊙ Sun-Fri 8.30am-12.30pm & 3.30-7.30pm

Trois (3, H8)
For the most exclusive in Fortuny fabrics made with original printing methods you have really only one choice and that is this modest looking outlet. At €240 per metre it's a steal!
✉ Campo San Maurizio, San Marco 2666 ☎ 041 522 29 05 🚤 Vallaresso & San Marco: Nos 1, 3, 4, 82 & N ⊙ Mon 4-7.30pm, Tues-Sat 10am-1pm & 4-7.30pm

LEATHER & SHOES

Gianni Baldan (3, E5)
In this unprepossessing little store in the shadow of the great Frari church, you can be sure of a range of good value classic leather shoes for men and women.
✉ Salizzada San Rocco, San Polo 3047 ☎ 041 528 75 01 🚤 San Tomà: Nos 1, 82 & N ⊙ Mon-Sat 9am-1pm & 3-7.30pm

Il Grifone (3, E2)
A virtually decor-free shopfront disguises this one-man leather workshop where you can get to grips with quality handmade

bags, belts, wallets and other leather objects for quite reasonable prices.
✉ Fondamenta del Gaffaro, Dorsoduro 3516 ☎ 041 522 94 52 🚤 Piazzale Roma: Nos 1, 4, 41, 42, 51, 52, 61, 62, 71, 72, 82 & N ⊙ Mon-Sat 10am-7.30pm

Manuela Calzature (3, D10) This is a small shoe shop with a good range, including more expensive footwear that they make under their own name. Don't judge it by the cheap junk outside.
✉ Calle del Galizzi, San Polo 1046 ☎ 041 522 66 52 🚤 San Silvestro: No 1 ⊙ 9am-7.30pm

Patrizia (3, D9)
Leather bags of all sorts, sizes and colours are the specialisation here. You can check out classy briefcases for the work front or elegant handbags for the evening.
✉ Campo Aponal, San Polo 1077
☎ 041 522 66 71 🚤 San Silvestro: No 1 ⊙ Mon-Sat 8am-1pm & 3-7pm

Fashionable Retail Therapy
Fashion fiends should head for the streets just west of St Mark's Square for (among others):

- **Armani** Calle dei Fabbri 989 (3, F12; ☎ 041 523 78 08)
- **Dolce & Gabbana** Calle Vallaresso 1313 (3, H12; ☎ 041 520 57 33)
- **Fendi** Salizzada San Moisè 1474 (3, H11; ☎ 041 520 57 33)
- **Gucci** Calle Vallaresso 1317 (3, J12; ☎ 041 520 74 84)
- **Kenzo** Ramo Fuseri 1814 (3, G11; ☎ 041 520 57 33)
- **Laura Biagiotti** Calle Larga XXII Marzo 2400 (3, H10; ☎ 041 520 34 01)
- **Missoni** Calle Vallaresso 1312/b (3, H12; ☎ 041 520 57 33)
- **Prada** Salizzada San Moisè 1464-1469 (3, H11; ☎ 041 528 39 66)
- **Versace** Campo San Moisè 1462 (3, H11; ☎ 041 520 00 57)

GLASS & CRYSTAL

If people think of shopping in Venice they tend to think of Murano glass. There are workshops and showrooms in the city and on Murano, but it is on the latter that you can see glass being blown (look for the sign *fornace*).

Barovier & Toso
(2, A11) Your chequebook will tremble as you enter this little temple of artistic glassware, connected with the Galleria Marina Barovier in San Marco. But you're not obliged to buy, and the displays allow you to appreciate top flight glass creations.
✉ **Fondamenta dei Vetrai 28, Murano**
☎ 041 527 43 85;
ℯ www.barovier.com
🚊 Colonna: Nos 41, 42, 71 & 72 ⏰ Mon-Sat 10am-12.30pm & 1-6pm

Berengo (2, A12)
Here is a purveyor of glass that has long abandoned any pretence at functionality in its products. This is glass for art's sake. If you are into the idea of glass as sculpture, this is one of a couple of places that could interest you.
✉ **Fondamenta dei Vetrai 109/a, Murano**
☎ 041 527 63 64
🚊 Colonna: Nos 41, 42, 71 & 72 ⏰ 10am-6pm

L'Isola's vivid glassware

Berengo Collection
(3, F13) If Murano is an island too far and you have an interest in glass as modern art, then you can pop in to this luxury showroom. It continues the theme of the Murano gallery and, while not everything may appeal, the pieces on show are certainly spectacular.
✉ **Calle Larga San Marco, San Marco 412-413** ☎ 041 241 07 63
🚊 Vallaresso & San Marco: Nos 1, 3, 4, 82 & N ⏰ 10am-6pm

Galleria Marina Barovier (3, G7)
Marina Barovier is one of the key names in quality Murano glass, and this store is a handy outlet for assessing just how expensive exquisite pieces can be. Wander in to see the latest creations of some of the most outstanding glass artists in Venice.
✉ **Calle delle Carrozze, San Marco 3216** ☎ 041 522 61 02 🚊 San Samuele: Nos 1, 3, 4, 82 & N ⏰ Tues-Sat 9.30am-12.30pm & 3.30-7.30pm

Galleria Rossella Junck (3, G8)
Those whose interests in glass are more historical than contemporary should try this gallery, which specialises in pieces made in Murano from the 16th to the 19th centuries. Objects range from mirrors to figurines to goblets and decorative plates.
✉ **Calle delle Botteghe, San Marco 3463** ☎ 041

528 65 37 🚊 Santa Maria del Giglio: No 1 ⏰ Mon-Sat 10.30am-noon & 3.30-7pm

L'Isola (3, H11)
L'Isola has glass objects by Carlo Moretti that are much appreciated for their elegance and finesse. The prices aren't exactly low, however.
✉ **Campo San Moisè, San Marco 1468** ☎ 041 523 19 73 🚊 Vallaresso & San Marco: Nos 1, 3, 4, 82 & N ⏰ Mon-Sat 9am-1pm & 3.30-7.30pm

Venini (2, A12)
Venini is yet another location for browsing the top shelf stuff before wandering off to poke your nose into less exalted glass factories and shops. Again, independent wealth comes in handy.
✉ **Fondamenta dei Vetrai 47-50, Murano**
☎ 041 73 99 55
🚊 Colonna: Nos 41, 42, 71 & 72 ⏰ Mon-Sat 9.30am-5.30pm

Venini (3, G13)
If anything, Venini's San Marco outlet is more captivating than the Murano headquarters. In this showroom you can admire some daring pieces far removed from the sort of Baroque baubles you have probably espied elsewhere.
✉ **Piazzetta dei Leoncini, San Marco 314**
☎ 041 522 40 45
🚊 San Zaccaria: Nos 1, 6, 14, 41, 42, 51, 52, 71, 72, 82 & N ⏰ Mon-Sat 10am-7.30pm

Damien Simonis

FOOD & DRINK

Aliani (3, D10)
For an outstanding collection of cheeses and other delicatessen products, Aliani has long been a favoured gastronomic stop in the Rialto area. You will also find a range of wines and other products.
✉ **Ruga Vecchia di San Giovanni, San Polo 654** ☎ **041 522 49 13** 🚤 **Rialto: Nos 1, 4, 82 & N** ⏰ **Mon-Sat 8am-1pm & 5-7.30pm**

Caffè Costarica (4, D6)
Since 1930 the Marchi family have been importing coffee from Costa Rica and other coffee-producing countries. They toast it daily for your delectation. If you don't want to take any away, you can just sip on your favourite mix at the little bar.
✉ **Rio Terrà San Leonardo, Cannaregio 1337** ☎ **041 71 63 71** 🚤 **San Marcuola: Nos 1, 82 & N** ⏰ **Mon-Sat 8am-1pm & 3.30-7.30pm**

Drogheria Mascari
(3, C10) Not far from Aliani, the Drogheria Mascari is another Venetian foodies' classic.

Jars full of all sorts of goods, salty and sweet, are accompanied by a mouth watering range of sweets, including slabs of chocolate and nougat (especially in evidence around Christmas time).
✉ **Ruga degli Spezieri, San Polo 381** ☎ **041 522 97 62** 🚤 **Rialto: Nos 1, 4, 82 & N** ⏰ **Wed 8am-1pm, Thurs-Tues 8am-1pm & 4-7.30pm**

Giacomo Rizzo (3, C12)
This place, just north of the post office, has been keeping the locals in pasta since 1905. Take a look if you want to buy handmade pastas – they produce quite a range (all made of natural products) including silly pasta, for instance Curaçao blue tagliatelle. You'll find anything from *tagliolini con curry indiano* to *tagliolini con*

cacao amaro (with bitter cocoa). They also sell imported specialities, such as olive oil from Modena and some pastas from Puglia.
✉ **Salizzada San Giovanni Crisostomo, Cannaregio 5778** ☎ **041 522 28 24** 🚤 **Rialto: Nos 1, 4, 82 & N** ⏰ **Thurs-Tues 8.30am-1pm & 3.30-6.30pm, Wed 8.30am-1pm**

Volpe Panetteria
(4, C4) This bakery and delicatessen in the heart of the Ghetto is not particularly special except for the fact that, alongside standard goods, it sells kosher food and wine.
✉ **Calle del Ghetto Vecchio, Cannaregio 1142** ☎ **041 71 51 78** 🚤 **Guglie: Nos 41, 42, 51 & 52** ⏰ **Thurs-Tues 8am-7pm**

Drogheria Mascari's got a lotti biscotti.

MARKETS

Fish Market (Pescaria)
(3, B10) Underneath the neo-Gothic roof built at the beginning of the 20th century, the fish market gets a mixed clientele of domestic shoppers and restaurateurs in search of ingredients for the day's menu. They have been sell-

ing fish here for 700 years.
✉ **Pescaria, Rialto, San Polo** 🚤 **traghetto from Campo Santa Sofia or vaporetto Rialto: Nos 1, 82 & N** ⏰ **7am-2pm**

Mercatino dei Miracoli (3, B13)
This is a bric-a-brac market

held in two adjacent squares. You can turn up all sorts of odds and ends and the atmosphere is always fun. It's also held at Via G Garibaldi (2, H12).
✉ **Campo San Canciano & Campo Santa Maria Nova** ☎ **041 274 73 15 (information)**

🏛 **Ca' d'Oro: Nos 1 & N**
🕐 2nd or 3rd weekend every month

Mercatino dell'Antiquariato
(3, H8) This antique market sets up three times yearly. You can find all sorts of stuff here. It's a little hard to plan a visit around the market since it happens so infrequently (in Apr, Sept and Dec in 2001).
✉ **Campo San Maurizio, San Marco** ☎ **041 45 41 76** (information)

🏛 **Santa Maria del Giglio: No 1**

Rialto Produce Markets **(3, C11)**
The raucous cries of vendors rise above the general hubbub of canny shoppers rubbing shoulders with unsuspecting tourists wandering into the area for the first time. A local favourite item is the artichoke, which the Venetians consider heavenly.
✉ **Rialto, San Polo**
🏛 **traghetto from**

Campo Santa Sofia or vaporetto Rialto: Nos 1, 82 & N 🕐 **7am-2pm**

Pesce! Pesce!

PAPER & STATIONERY

Venice is noted for its *carta marmorizzata* (marbled paper). It has become something of a hit with visitors and is used for all sorts of things, from expensive gift wrap to book covers.

Cartavenezia **(3, C7)**
A curious little place hidden along a narrow street, Cartavenezia has objects of every possible type made of a rough white paper, clearly fragile and with a purely decorative vocation.
✉ **Calle Longa, Santa Croce 2125** ☎ **041 524 12 83** 🏛 **San Stae: Nos 1 & N**
🕐 Mon 3.30-7.30pm, Tues-Sat 11am-1pm & 3.30-7.30pm

Il Papiro **(3, H8)**
A bright, spacious stationers, Il Papiro doesn't pretend to compete with the traditional paper shops. Among a modest selection of such items you will also find anything from elegant envelopes to letter openers.
✉ **Calle del Piovan, San Marco 2764** ☎ **041 522 30 55**
🏛 **Santa Maria del Giglio: No 1** 🕐 **Mon-Sat 10am-7.30pm, Sun 10.30am-7pm**

Il Pavone **(3, K8)**
The dominant colours (blues, reds and yellows) and motifs (floral shapes, cherubs and others) at Il Pavone change from one day to the other. The templates are applied equally to hand-printed paper as well as to ties and other objects. You can have T-shirts made here too.
✉ **Fondamenta Venier dai Leoni, Dorsoduro 721** ☎ **041 523 45 17**
🏛 **Accademia: Nos 1, 3, 4, 82 & N** 🕐 **9.30am-1.30pm & 2.30-7.30pm**

Legatoria Polliero
(3, E6) Here is another traditional exponent of the art of Venetian bookbinding with (and without) marbled paper. You barely have room to stand when you penetrate this den, with piles of leather-bound books, paper-bound folders, and all sorts of other stationery piled higgledy-piggledy high to the rafters.
✉ **Campo dei Frari, San Polo 2995** ☎ **041 528 51 30** 🏛 **San Tomà: Nos 1, 82 & N**
🕐 **9.30am-1.30pm & 2.30-7.30pm**

Ripped Off?
Feel you have been ripped off? Received lousy service in a hotel or restaurant? You could try calling Venice No Problem on ☎ **800 35 59 20**. The toll free number is manned by multilingual staff in conjunction with the Venice Tourist Board (APT) and, depending on your situation, may be able to help.

Damien Simonis

FOR CHILDREN

The Disney Store
(3, D12) All right, perhaps you'll think it's as bad as mentioning McDonald's. Fact is, kids love Disney toys and this place may well save a failing parental relationship with loved little ones.
✉ **Campo San Bartolomeo, San Marco 5257**
☎ **041 522 39 80**
🚤 **Rialto: Nos 1, 4, 82 & N** ⏲ **10am-8pm**

Gilberto Penzo (3, E6)
See p. 68.

Il Baule Blu (3, E6)
Come here for a luxury bear. The owners of this shop have turned cuddly bears into a business for aficionados. If you've

brought your own along to Venice, you can rest easy knowing that the shop also operates a Teddy Hospital.
✉ **Campo San Tomà, San Polo 2916/a**
☎ **041 71 94 48** 🚤 **San Tomà: Nos 1, 82 & N** ⏲ **Mon-Sat 10am-12.30pm & 4-7.30pm**

Jallits (3, B8)
This is a fun and original little shop with items that

might interest the kiddies, such as pencils topped by little animals, decorative pandas and rabbits that look more like brushes, toy wooden trains like they used to make, as well as general household bric-a-brac.
✉ **Ramo Santa Maria Mater Domini, Santa Croce 2268/a** ☎ **041 71 37 51** 🚤 **San Stae: Nos 1 & N** ⏲ **11am-1.30pm & 3-7.30pm**

It's Sale Time!
Time your visit to coincide with the sales and you may pick up some great bargains. Winter sales run from early January to mid-February and the summer sales run from July to early September. Look for the *saldi* signs.

SPECIALIST STORES

Codognato (3, H12)
Possibly the city's best known jewellery shop, Codognato has classic pieces that have attracted the likes of Jackie Onassis.
✉ **Calle Seconda dell'Ascensione, San Marco 1295** ☎ **041 522 50 42** 🚤 **Vallaresso & San Marco: Nos 1, 3, 4, 82 & N** ⏲ **Mon 4-7pm, Tues-Sun 10am-1pm & 4-7pm**

Guarinoni (3, E6)
Although you are not likely to haul a boatload of furniture back home from Venice, it's always nice to look. Guarinoni, where restoration is also done, enjoys a generous space to show off fine polished timber furniture, ranging from dining tables to night tables.
✉ **Campo San Tomà, San Polo 2862**

☎ **041 523 12 59**
🚤 **San Tomà: Nos 1, 82 & N** ⏲ **8am-12.30pm & 3-7pm**

Le Botteghe della Solidarietà (3, D11)
Part of a series of 'solidarity' stores across the country, you can find everything from health foods and coffee imported from the developing world, to drums, pipes and other instruments from various African and South American countries.
✉ **Salizzada Pio X, San Marco 5164** ☎ **041 522 75 45** 🚤 **Rialto: Nos 1, 4, 82 & N** ⏲ **Mon-Sat 10am-1pm & 4-7pm**

Lush (3, A10)
Handmade soaps and fragrances with a whiff of fresh fruit is the order of

the day in this fine-smelling chain store. Some look like chocolates, others like cricket balls. All promise olfactory pleasure.
✉ **Strada Nova, Cannaregio 3822**
☎ **041 24 11 20**
🚤 **Ca' d'Oro: Nos 1, 41, 42, 51, 52, 61, 82 & N** ⏲ **Tues-Sat 10am-1pm & 4-7.30pm**

Mille e Una Nota
(3, D9) If during your stay in Venice you require strings for your guitar, or would like to acquire some new panpipes, a shiny new mouth organ or perhaps even a harp, this is the place to come to.
✉ **Calle del Mezzo, San Polo 1235** ☎ **041 523 18 22** 🚤 **San Silvestro: No 1** ⏲ **Mon-Sat 9.30am-1pm & 3-7.30pm**

places to eat

Can one eat well in Venice? Ask an Italian and you may be greeted by a contemptuous snort. Dining out is doubtless more expensive than elsewhere in Italy and palming off second rate food onto unwitting tourists seems to be a Venetian sport.

But enough places, from the modest *osteria* (traditional bar/restaurant) serving snacks and wine to the impeccable luxury of Harry's Bar, make up a healthy exception to the rule. After all, they have the locals to satisfy too.

Eating, Italian Style

Colazione (breakfast) is generally a quick affair, a warm cappuccino with a croissant or other pastry had on the hop in a bar on the way to work.

Pranzo (lunch) is traditionally the main meal of the day and most shops and offices close for two or three hours around midday to accommodate it. *Cena*, the evening meal, used to be a light supper, but globalisation of the Western work ethic seems to be changing that.

A full meal consists of an antipasto (starter), followed by the *primo piatto*, usually pasta, risotto or soup, and a *secondo* of fish or meat. You order a *contorno* (side of vegetables or salad) separately. Meals finish with a *dolce* (dessert), *gelato* (ice cream) or fruit and *caffè*.

As a rule restaurants open 12.30-3pm but often stop taking orders after 2pm. Evening dining starts at 7.30pm with few places serving after 10.30pm.

Il Conto (The Bill)

The price ranges used here indicate the cost per person of a two course meal, including a bottle of modest wine:

$	up to €15
$$	€16-29
$$$	€30-50
$$$$	over €50

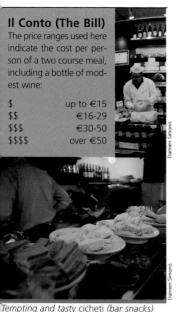

Damien Simons

Tempting and tasty cicheti *(bar snacks)*

Sidestepping Bad Salad

Steer clear of restaurants along tourist thoroughfares (such as the Lista di Spagna) advertising impossibly cheap three-course menus. Touts and multi-language menus are also a sign you will be treated to sloppy microwaved impersonations of food. Watch out for the tour groups scoffing tired salad and droopy pasta.

Where to Eat

For *cicheti* (bar snacks) and local wine Venetians traditionally seek out a *bacaro* or *osteria*. The latter can also be an inn offering a limited menu of simple food and house wines. A trattoria is traditionally a family-run no frills restaurant, while a *ristorante* was always a self-consciously more upmarket option. These terms can be used as a guide, but the distinction between them is increasingly blurred.

Cuisine of a Maritime Empire

The kitchens of Venice have for centuries been filled with the aromas of the sea. The wider Veneto is a different story. The farther inland you go, the more meat dominates. Anyone who does not like seafood may stress a little in Venice as many restaurants offer nothing much else.

A peculiarly Venetian habit is the bar snack, reminiscent of Spanish *tapas*. Known as *cicheti*, they are often made up of all sorts of deep-fried watery critters. They can also make their way to restaurant tables as antipasti. Among them are *sarde in saor*, pilchards fried up in an onion marinade. *Baccalà* (salt cod) is popular in various forms, such as *baccalà mantecato*, prepared in garlic and parsley. *Granseole* (crabs) and other shellfish abound.

Classic primi include *risi e bisi*, a rice and pea concoction, and the central Mediterranean fave, *pasta e fagioli* (pasta and fava beans prepared as a kind of stew). *Risotto*, rice-based dishes that can contain seafood and other ingredients, is typical of the Veneto. *Zuppa di pesce* (fish soup) and *bigoli alla busara* (a local version of spaghetti with scampi and a mild red sauce) are common.

In Venice, fish of all types dominate main courses. Meat dishes *are* available, although often choices are limited. *Polenta*, a corn based stodge that is to the Veneto what couscous is to North Africans, often accompanies dishes. On its own it is indescribably bland!

Those with a sweet tooth might finish with *tiramisù*, a rich dessert in mascarpone that was supposedly cooked up in Venice. Many prefer to end with a *sgroppino*, lemon sorbet with a splash of vodka (and sometimes a little sparkling white wine) and a drop of milk, in a wine glass.

There are no real vegetarian restaurants although you should be able to get by with the many vegetable cicheti, salads and side orders. And of course several pasta dishes come with vegetable sauces.

Most wine you will drink in Venice comes from the surrounding Veneto region and neighbouring regions that make up the Triveneto area, Trentino-Alto Adige and Friuli-Venezia Giulia. A Venetian wanting a quick drink in a bar is likely to ask for a *prosecco*, a light bubbly white wine produced all over the Veneto. Some good drops are produced around Verona, including Soave (white), Valpolicella (red) and Bardolino (red and rosé). Pinot Grigio (white) and Pinot Nero (red) from Friuli are promising. *Grappa*, the transparent firewater made from grapes, comes from the Grappa area in the Veneto – it is great as an after dinner digestive or to fire up your shot of coffee.

Ward off a rumbling tum Venetian style, with snacks from the sea

SAN MARCO

Tourist traps abound, but sprinkled in between are some wonderful spots.

Enoteca Il Volto
(3, E10) **$$**
Wine Bar
Near Campo San Luca, this spot has an excellent wine selection and a tempting array of snacks, which will no doubt induce you to hang about for more than one glass.
✉ **Calle Cavalli 4081**
☎ **041 522 89 45**
🚏 **Rialto: Nos 1, 4, 82 & N** 🕓 **Mon-Sat 12-3pm & 7-10.30pm**

Harry's Bar
(3, J12) **$$$$**
Restaurant/Bar
The Cipriani family, who started this bar in 1931, claims to have invented many Venetian specialities, including the Bellini cocktail. On the culinary side, they also claim the patent for *carpaccio* (very fine slices of raw meat). The quality of the meal may not live up to the price or the expectations, but this *is* Harry's after all. Toscanini, Chaplin, Hemingway and just about everyone who was anyone (and quite a few who were definitely

Fine dining at da Ivo

Damien Simonis

no-one) have eaten and drunk here. See also p. 95.
✉ **Calle Vallaresso 1323** ☎ **041 528 57 77**
🚏 **Vallaresso & San Marco: Nos 1, 3, 4, 82 & N** 🕓 **12-11pm**

Osteria al Bacareto
(3, G7) **$$**
Osteria/Trattoria
The search for a good traditional trattoria in this corner of San Marco is over when you reach al Bacareto. Since it doubles as an osteria, you can opt for a plateful of cicheti with a glass of wine.
✉ **Calle Crosera 3447**
☎ **041 528 93 36**
🚏 **San Samuele: Nos 1, 3, 4, 82 & N** 🕓 **Mon-Fri 12.30-2.30pm & 7-10pm** ♿

Ristorante al Gazzettino
(3, E12) **$$$**
Restaurant
Since 1953, this restaurant, below the *pensione* (guesthouse) of the same name, has been a well known favourite in central Venice. Until 1977, journos and printers from *Il Gazzettino* newspaper, then based in the nearby Ca' Faccanon, made it their regular. As if in tribute to the good ol' days, the present owners have plastered the walls with pages from *Il Gazzettino* past – if you can read Italian, you'll find it hard not to let your food go cold.
✉ **Calle di Mezzo 4971**
☎ **041 522 33 14**
🚏 **Rialto: Nos 1, 4, 82 & N** 🕓 **Tues-Sun 12-3pm & 7.30-10.30pm** ♿

> ### It's the Business
> Need to do some serious business munching? Try:
>
> Al Covo (p. 86)
> Da Fiore (p. 82)
> Fiaschetteria Toscana (p. 84)
> Ristorante da Ivo (p. 80)
> Vecio Fritolin (p. 83)

Ristorante da Ivo
(3, G11) **$$$**
Restaurant
A Venetian dining classic, at da Ivo you will have a choice of seafood, predictably the house speciality, and a selection of Venetian and Tuscan meat dishes, all washed down with a fine range of wines. The atmosphere is quietly elegant and your choice of dish and wine can easily send your bill into the deluxe category.
✉ **Calle dei Fuseri 1809** ☎ **041 528 50 04**
🚏 **Rialto: Nos 1, 4, 82 & N** 🕓 **Mon-Sat 12.30-3pm & 7-11pm**

Vino Vino (3, H10) **$**
Bar/Osteria
This is a popular and long standing little den of palate pleasure just over Ponte Veste, near the now scorched Teatro La Fenice. The menu changes daily and they regularly serve up such Venetian faves as sarde in saor. There is a good selection of vegetables. Wine is sold by the glass for €1.05.
✉ **Calle del Cafetier 2007** ☎ **041 523 70 27**
🚏 **Santa Maria del Giglio: No 1** 🕓 **Wed-Mon 12.30-3pm & 7-11pm** V

DORSODURO

Somewhat removed from the main tourist bustle, you can prise all sorts of gems from Dorsoduro's nooks and crannies.

Ai Gondolieri
(3, K8)   **$$$**
Restaurant
Surrounded as it is by innu-merable seafood restaur-ants, Ai Gondolieri comes as a welcome change for red-blooded carnivores. All mains are land-going crit-ters (such as Angus steak, duck and liver). Dishes can be accompanied by a select offering of wine. If you opt for all courses you will bust the €50 mark.
✉ **Fondamenta Ospe-daleto 366** ☎ **041 528 63 96** ⚐ **Accademia: Nos 1, 3, 4, 82 & N** ⊙ **Wed-Mon 12.30-3pm & 7.30-10pm**

Antica Locanda
Montin (3, J4)   **$$**
Restaurant
This place, which will appeal to gourmands, has generally good food and a shady garden. They offer some fine wines too.
✉ **Fondamenta di Borgo 1147** ☎ **041 522 71 51** ⚐ **Ca' Rezzonico: No 1** ⊙ **Thurs-Tues 12.30-2.30pm & 7.30-11pm**

Arca (3, F4)   **$**
Pizzeria/Restaurant
On Tuesday nights there's live music here, usually of a light jazz variety to accom-pany your cheap and cheerful chow, which attracts a predominantly student clientele. You can start with a vegetable soup at €5 or seafood first course for around €9. They are OK but the place is best for its pizzas (€4.50-8), including a couple of

sweet versions, one with Nutella and the other with citrus fruit!
✉ **Calle San Pantalon 3757** ☎ **041 524 22 36** ⚐ **San Tomà: Nos 1, 82 & N** ⊙ **Mon-Sat 12.30-3pm & 7pm-midnight**

L'Incontro (3, G4)   **$$**
Restaurant
Typical regional fare is served at this quiet, inti-mate restaurant. The menu alters daily.
✉ **Rio Terrà Canal 3062** ☎ **041 522 24 04** ⚐ **Ca' Rezzonico: No 1** ⊙ **Tues-Sun 12.30-3pm & 7.30-1am** ⚐

Osteria ai Carmini
(3, H3)   **$$$**
Osteria
For fresh fish and seafood, this is a good spot to seek out. It is an unpretentious and tiny little place, where you could also drop by to munch on an array of cicheti.
✉ **Calle delle Pazienze 2894/a** ☎ **041 523 11 15** ⚐ **Ca' Rezzonico: No 1** ⊙ **Mon-Sat 9.30am-11pm**

Osteria da Toni
(3, J1)   **$$**
Osteria
This is a popular workers' haunt, where you can eat good seafood at relatively low prices or just sip wine. When the sun shines, take your place by the canal. Otherwise, elbow your way inside to the rough-and-tumble tables.
✉ **Fondamenta San Basilio 1642**

☎ **041 528 68 99** ⚐ **San Basilio: Nos 61, 62, 82 & N** ⊙ **Tues-Sun 11.30am-2pm & 7-10pm**

Riviera (3, K2)   **$$$**
Restaurant
Dine by candlelight on the broadwalk that looks across to Giudecca. Even on sunny winter days they optimistically get the tables out for lunch when you might be better off dining in the warm, exposed brick interior. Try the *risotto del giorno* as a first course, after which you have a choice from about a dozen seafood and meat mains. Or you can drop by for breakfast.
✉ **Fondamenta Zattere al Ponte Lungo 1473** ☎ **041 522 76 21** ⚐ **San Basilio: Nos 61, 62, 82 & N** ⊙ **Tues-Sat 12.30-2.30pm & 7-11pm, Sun 12.30-2.30pm**

Romantic ReTreats

Lovers love Venice. And good food in the right place can be the per-fect aphrodisiac. A few locations you might con-sider include:

All'Altanella (p. 87)
Al Covo (p. 86)
Da Fiore (p. 82)
Harry's Bar (p. 80)
L'Incontro (p. 81)
Locanda Cipriani (p. 88)
Riviera (p 81)
Vini da Gigio (p. 85)

SAN POLO

From conspiratorial cicheti to understated high cuisine and on to Indian, San Polo is full of surprises.

You'll find good value and authenticity at All'Arco.

All'Arco (3, C10) $$$
Osteria
For good value cicheti and a glass of wine or two, this is one of the most authentic *osterie* in the San Polo area. People gather around the bar or, on warmer days, huddle together on stools by little tables in among the hubbub of the cramped lanes near the Rialto.
✉ Calle Arco 436
☎ 041 520 56 66
🛥 San Silvestro: No 1
🕐 Mon-Sat 12-2pm
& 7.30-10.30pm

Cantina Do Mori (3, C10) $$
Osteria
Hidden away near the Ponte di Rialto, this is something of a traditional institution. Unfortunately, the local consensus is that the prices have gone up unreasonably. Shame, because it is an enticing place, oozing history and still attracting a lot of local custom for such items as its *francobolli* ('stamps'), tiny little stuffed bread snacks.
✉ Sotoportego dei do Mori 429 ☎ 041 522 54 01 🛥 San Stae: Nos 1 & N 🕐 Mon-Sat 12-3pm & 7.30-11pm

Cantina Do Spade (3, C9) $$$
Osteria
Welcome to Venice's oldest eating house, where the emphasis is more on the full meals than hanging about the bar for snacks. Still, you can eat a range of bruschetta (hardly a Venetian idea but tasty nonetheless). The place is worth a try although it shows signs of slipping down the tourist slope.
✉ Calle do Spade 860
☎ 041 521 05 74
🛥 San Stae: Nos 1 & N
🕐 Mon-Sat 12-2.30pm
& 7.30-10.30pm

Da Fiore (3, C7) $$$$
Restaurant
Da Fiore is the only recipient of a Michelin star in Venice. The unprepossessing shopfront appearance belies an Art Deco interior and some fine traditional dishes, such as *risotto di scampi*, prepared with optimum care. The place can easily be booked out for dinner weeks in advance. It's easier to get in for lunch.
✉ Calle del Scaleter 2202 ☎ 041 72 13 08 🛥 San Stae: Nos 1 & N 🕐 Tues-Sat 12-2.30pm & 7.30-11pm

Ganesh Ji (3, C5) $$
Indian
Fancy a quick curry? Forget it. But a good slow one can be had on the pleasant little canalside terrace of this place. Danilo and his charmingly chaotic staff serve up authentic dishes at reasonable prices – pleased guests have scribbled their appreciation on the walls. You can takeaway.
✉ Fondamenta Rio Marin 2426 ☎ 041 71 90 84 🛥 Ferrovia: Nos 1, 3, 4, 41, 42, 51, 52, 71, 72, 82 & N 🕐 Thurs-Tues 12-3pm & 7.30pm-midnight Ⓥ

Osteria alla Patatina (3, E7) $$$
Osteria
Pile in around the rough timber tables and benches for some cicheti or simple pasta dishes, well washed down with a couple of glasses of robust red wine. The Potato Crisp Inn, as it is called, makes no compromise with fickle trends and retains a traditional air.
✉ Calle Saoneri 2741/a
☎ 041 523 72 38
🛥 San Tomà: Nos 1, 82 & N 🕐 Mon-Fri 12-2.30pm & 7.30-10.30pm, Sat 12-2.30pm

Traditional treats at Patatina

SANTA CROCE

A handful of places are worth bearing in mind around here.

Al Nono Risorto
(3, C8) $$$
Pizzeria/Restaurant
We'd recommend you stop in here if only to luxuriate in the leafy canalside garden in summertime. In the cooler months customers head inside the lofty timber dining area. The pizzas in particular are very good. Otherwise you could opt for a reasonable set price lunch menu (€15). The service is friendly if a little scatty.
✉ **Sotoportego de Siora Bettina, Santa Croce 2338** ☎ **041 524 11 69** 🚤 **San Stae: Nos 1 & N** 🕐 **Thurs-Tues 12-3pm & 7-11pm** ♿

Al Prosecco (3, B6) $$
Osteria
This is a friendly and bustling osteria. The idea here is to prop up the bar, order a selection of cicheti and wash them down with, well, *prosecco* (p. 79) It is one of the best spots of its ilk in the area.x
✉ **Campo di San Giacomo dell'Orio 1503** ☎ **041 524 02 22** 🚤 **San Stae: Nos 1 & N** 🕐 **Mon-Sat 11.30am-2.30pm & 7-10pm**

Antica Besseta
(3, B5) $$$
Trattoria
In the graceful rear dining area of this trattoria are real tablecloths (not the rough paper place mats in vogue elsewhere), discrete lighting, old-world crystal glasses and a tasty seafood menu. The *tagliolini alla salsa di gamberi e zucchine* (thin tagliatelle in a shrimp and courgette sauce) is light and full of shrimps! Accompanying it with a Valpolicella makes for a great meal.
✉ **Salizzada de Ca' Zusto, Santa Croce 1395** ☎ **041 72 16 87** 🚤 **Riva de Biasio: Nos 1 & N** 🕐 **Thurs-Mon 12-2.30pm & 7-10.30pm, Wed 7-10.30pm** ♿

Osteria La Zucca
(3, A7) $$$
Mediterranean
It seems like just another Venetian trattoria, but the menu (which changes daily) is an enticing mix of Mediterranean themes. The vegetable side orders (around €3.50) alone are inspired (try the *pepperonata alle melanzane*, a cool stew of capsicum and aubergine), while the mains (€12) are substantial. You won't need to order pasta as well.
✉ **Calle del Tintor 1762** ☎ **041 524 15 70** 🚤 **San Stae: Nos 1 & N** 🕐 **Mon-Sat 12-2pm & 7-11pm** Ⓥ

Trattoria al Ponte
(3, A6) $$
Trattoria
Arrive early here and try to grab one of the few canalside tables. This simple, rustic eatery tends to specialise in fish, but other options are available. The food quality is reliable and the prices reasonable.
✉ **Ponte del Megio 1666** ☎ **041 71 97 77** 🚤 **San Stae: Nos 1 & N** 🕐 **Mon-Fri 12.30-2pm & 7-10.30pm, Sat 12.30-2pm**

Vecio Fritolin
(3, B8) $$$
Restaurant
A *fritolin* was traditionally a kind of seafood and polenta takeaway. At this one you can now sit down to meticulous cooking, with local and Italian dishes. The *pappardelle con scampi e fagioli* (broad ribbon pasta with prawns and white beans) is an enticing first course.
✉ **Calle della Regina 226** ☎ **041 522 28 81** 🚤 **San Stae: Nos 1 & N** 🕐 **Tues-Sat 12-3pm & 7.30-11pm, Sun 12-3pm** Ⓥ

Damien Simonis

Grab some canalside seats and watch the tide of events.

CANNAREGIO

There are loads of *osterie* and even a few foreign options to choose from in Cannaregio.

Alla Fontana
(4, C4)   **$$**
Osteria
Close to the Jewish ghetto, this little osteria has been serving local tipplers for more than 100 years. For many it is a place to chat over house wine (all of it from the surrounding Veneto and Friuli regions), cold meats and cheese. They also offer a limited menu of mains.
☒ **Fondamenta di Cannaregio 1102 ☎ 041 71 50 77 ⚓ Guglie: Nos 41, 42, 51 & 52** ⏰ **Tues-Sat 12-2.30pm & 7.30-11pm**

Anice Stellato
(4, A6)   **$$$**
Trattoria
Awaiting you in the guise of doorman is a huge *damigiana* (demijohn) by the entrance. Inside, the heavy timber tables and wooden chairs are perfect for a chatty, convivial meal. The pasta dishes are excellent and the mains imaginative, including the occasional use of curry and other spices not immediately

associated with either local or national cuisine.
☒ **Fondamenta della Sensa 3272 ☎ 041 72 07 44 ⚓ Madonna dell'Orto: Nos 41, 42, 51 & 52** ⏰ **Tues-Sun 12-2.30pm & 7-11pm** ⚕

Cantina Vecia Carbonera
(4, D8)   **$$**
Osteria
They've retained the wood panelling from the days when this was simply a place to stop by for a drink. It's been spruced up and you can now opt for some tasty cicheti or a full sit-down meal. They occasionally organise a little music.
☒ **Ponte Sant'Antonio 2329 ☎ 041 71 03 76 ⚓ San Marcuola: Nos 1, 82 & N** ⏰ **Tues-Sun 12-2.30pm & 7.30pm-midnight**

Da Marisa
(4, B1)   **$$**
Trattoria
They are not especially fond of tourists here so you may need to work up some Italian credentials to squeeze in. Expect robust meat-based cooking

(Da Marisa is near the former abattoir but seems to have taken no notice of its demise).
☒ **Fondamenta di San Giobbe 652/b ☎ 041 72 02 11 ⚓ Tre Archi: Nos 41, 42, 51 & 52** ⏰ **Thurs-Tues 12-2pm & 8-10.30pm (closed Sun lunch)**

Fiaschetteria Toscana
(3, C12)   **$$$**
Restaurant
A classic that has long-maintained quality, this place is about as Tuscan as a gondola. They serve up solid Venetian food to be washed down with a choice of wines from an impressive list that includes tipples from around the country. The *frittura della Serenissima*, a mixed fried seafood platter, is memorable.
☒ **Salizzada San Giovanni Crisostomo 5719 ☎ 041 528 52 81 ⚓ Ca' d'Oro: Nos 1 & N** ⏰ **Mon 12-3pm, Wed-Sun 12-3pm & 7.30-10.30pm**

Gam Gam
(4, C4)   **$$**
Kosher/Mediterranean
Gam Gam is great for your taste buds if you like Israeli-style felafels and other Middle Eastern delicacies. This place is fully kosher and presents a diverse menu, ranging from Red Sea spaghetti to couscous (with choice of meat, fish or vegetable sauce) and from houmous to that arch-Venetian side order of *fondi di carciofi* (artichoke hearts).
☒ **Calle del Ghetto**

Squeeze in and snack on at Ostaria al Ponte (p. 85).

Damien Simons

Vecchio 1123 ☎ 041 71 52 84 ⚓ Guglie: Nos 41, 42, 51 & 52 🕙 Sun-Thurs 12-10pm, Fri 12-2.30pm ♿ **V**

Ostaria al Ponte
(3, C14) $$
Osteria
This aptly named and highly recommended snack place is on the 'frontier' with Sestiere di Castello. Almost claustrophobically small, it is a well regarded stop where you can nibble on cicheti and indulge in good wines.
✉ **Calle Larga G Gallina 6378** ☎ **041 528 61 57** ⚓ Fondamente Nuove: Nos 12, 13, 41, 42, 51 & 52 🕙 Mon-Sat 8am-3.30pm & 4.30-8.30pm

Osteria alla Frasca
(3, A14) $$$
Restaurant
The dishes on offer are fairly standard, favouring seafood and they're also a smidge pricey for what you get. However, the setting, with tables spilling out into the charming *campiello*, rarely touched by tourist caravans, is a winner. The locals like it too and you'll often see a few chatting over an *ombra* (small glass of wine).
✉ **Corte della Carità 5176** ☎ **041 528 54 33** ⚓ Fondamente Nuove: Nos 12, 13, 41, 42, 51 & 52 🕙 12-2.30pm & 7.30-10.30pm ♿

Osteria da Alberto
(3, B14) $$
Osteria
Another hidden Venetian jewel, this place is run by Alberto, a well known figure in the business of serving up traditional food in Venice.

Be aware that they close the kitchen by about 9pm here. The baccalà is good.
✉ **Calle Larga G Gallina 5401** ☎ **041 523 81 53** ⚓ Ospedale Civile: Nos 41, 42, 51 & 52 🕙 Mon-Sat 12-2.30pm & 7.30-10pm

Osteria dalla Vedova
(3, A10) $$
Osteria
The 'Widow's Inn', off Strada Nova, is also called Trattoria Ca' d'Or and is one of the oldest osterie in Venice. The food, whether you nibble on the cicheti or settle in for a full (mostly seafood) meal, is good and modestly priced.
✉ **Calle del Pistor 3912** ☎ **041 528 53 24** ⚓ Ca' d'Oro: Nos 1 & N 🕙 Mon-Wed & Fri-Sat 12-2.30pm & 7.30-10.30pm

Paradiso Perduto
(4, C9) $$
Osteria/Bar
Young people will enjoy this spot, which frequently proffers live music and has tables outside in summer. The *lasagna ai carciofi* (artichoke lasagne) is great and the long list of cicheti is equally enticing. It gets pretty packed.
✉ **Fondamenta della Misericordia 2539** ☎ **041 72 05 81** ⚓ Madonna dell'Orto: Nos 41, 42, 51 & 52 🕙 Thurs-Sat & Mon-Tues 12-3pm & 7pm-midnight ♿ **V**

Sahara (4, C9) $$
Middle Eastern
At Sahara you can get a reasonable serving of Syrian food, with old favourites such as falafel, houmous, kebab meat and other delights. The food is not bad

Appetising antipast

and certainly makes a change. You may even get a display of belly-dancing thrown in.
✉ **Fondamenta della Misericordia 2520** ☎ **041 72 10 77** ⚓ Fondamente Nuove: Nos 12, 13, 41, 42, 51 & 52 🕙 Tues-Sun 12-2.30pm & 8pm-midnight ♿ **V**

Vini da Gigio
(3, A10) $$$
Restaurant
Gigio stocks a fine selection of reds and whites from the Veneto and beyond, and a trip here means good wine in the company of some excellent cooking. How about the *gnocchi con burro fuso e ricotta affumicata* (little dumplings bathed in melted butter and smoked ricotta cheese)?
✉ **Fondamenta della Chiesa 3628/a** ☎ **041 528 51 40** ⚓ Ca' d'Oro: Nos 1 & N 🕙 Tues-Sun 12-2.30pm & 7.30-11pm

CASTELLO

As you move east of the San Marco vortex, an array of interesting dining options for all pockets reveals itself.

Al Covo (2, G11) **$$$$**
Restaurant
Cooking at Al Covo is resolutely local and of a high quality. Inside the atmosphere is hushed and unpretentious and some of the seafood dishes in particular are divine. Credit cards are not accepted.
✉ **Campiello della Pescaria 3968** ☎ **041 522 38 12** 🚤 **San Zaccaria: Nos 1, 6, 14, 41, 42, 51, 52, 71, 72, 82 & N** ⏲ **Fri-Tues 12.30-3pm & 7.30-11pm**

Al Nuovo Galeon (2, H12) **$$$**
Restaurant
You can almost hear the creak of the hull as you wander into what seems like the innards of a great Venetian merchant ship. As usual the emphasis is on seafood and the place tends to fill quickly – it's advisable to book ahead.
✉ **Via G Garibaldi 1308** ☎ **041 520 46 56** 🚤 **Giardini: Nos 1, 41, 42, 51, 52, 61, 62, 82 & N** ⏲ **Wed-Sun 12.30-3pm & 7.30-11pm** ⚘

Al Portego (3, D13) **$$**
Osteria
Situated beneath the portico that gives this osteria its name, Al Portego is an inviting stop for cicheti and wine, along with some robust meals. Try the *bigoli* (thick, rough Venetian pasta), whatever sauce they come with.
✉ **Calle Malvasia** ☎ **041 522 90 38** 🚤 **Rialto: Nos 1, 4, 82**

& N ⏲ **Mon-Sat 12-2.30pm & 7.30-10.30pm**

Alle Testiere (3, E14) **$$$**
Trattoria
The chef may well come for a chat as you sample the tasty offerings in the cosy dining area here. Fish is the leitmotif. A handful of starters and pasta courses (all around €12) are followed by a couple of set mains or fresh fish. Round off with quality wines.
✉ **Calle del Mondo Nuovo, Castello 5801** ☎ **041 522 72 20** 🚤 **Rialto: Nos 1, 4, 82 & N** ⏲ **Tues-Sun 12-3pm & 7pm-midnight**

Hostaria da Franz (2, H13) **$$$**
Restaurant
If you end up in the eastern end of Castello, past the Arsenale, you will be in a distinct minority. The only spot in this neighbourhood really worth considering is this homely place. It specialises in crustaceous creatures.
✉ **Fondamenta San Giuseppe 755** ☎ **041 522 08 61** 🚤 **Giardini: Nos 1, 41, 42, 51, 52, 61, 62, 82 & N** ⏲ **Wed-Mon 12.30-3pm & 7.30-10.30pm** ⚘

La Mascareta (3, D15) **$$**
Osteria
A few steps away from the better known Mascaron (the 'big mask'; see below) is this 'little mask', a perfectly genial tavern for the

wine and a limited but tempting range of cicheti.
✉ **Calle Lunga di Santa Maria Formosa 5138** ☎ **041 523 07 44** 🚤 **Rialto: Nos 1, 4, 82 & N** ⏲ **Mon-Sat 12-2.30pm & 7.30-11pm**

Osteria al Mascaron (3, D15) **$$$**
Osteria
The interior here is all dark timber and low slung ceilings. At the bar you can indulge in a good range of cicheti, and a full meal is also an option in this nononsense environment.
✉ **Calle Lunga di Santa Maria Formosa 5525** ☎ **041 522 59 95** 🚤 **Rialto: Nos 1, 4, 82 & N** ⏲ **Mon-Sat 12.30-2.30pm & 7.30-10.30pm**

Tokyo Sushi Restaurant (3, E14) **$$**
Japanese
Don't get too excited as this is not exactly a fine sushi experience. It is, however, as close as you will get to it in Venice. The paucity of non-Italian dining options in Venice is reason enough to give it a mention.
✉ **Calle Casselleria 5281** ☎ **041 277 04 20** 🚤 **San Zaccaria: Nos 1, 6, 14, 41, 42, 51, 52, 71, 72, 82 & N** ⏲ **Mon 12-3pm, Tues-Sun 12-3pm & 7-11pm** ⚘ **V**

Trattoria agli Artisti (3, E15) **$**
Trattoria
If it's cheap and cheerful food you want, this trattoria

is an acceptable stop. It usually has two set menus that will keep body and soul together for a low cost. You can sit at the little tables and benches outside.

✉ **Ruga Giuffa 4625**
☎ **041 277 02 90**
🚣 **San Zaccaria: Nos 1, 6, 14, 41, 42, 51, 52, 71, 72, 82 & N**
🕐 **Thurs-Tues 12-3pm & 7-10.30pm** ♿

Foreign Eats

Opportunities for eating anything but Venetian or more broadly Italian food are limited in the lagoon city. Among the few options are:

Da Luca (p. 89)
Gam Gam (p. 84)
Ganesh Ji (p. 82)
Sahara (p. 85)
Tokyo Sushi Restaurant (p. 86)

Trattoria Corte Sconta (2, G11) $$$
Trattoria
A cosy eatery with the option of dining in the rear courtyard, Corte Sconta is hidden well off even the unbeaten track. The chefs prepare almost exclusively seafood classics, such as their delicious *risotto ai scampi*. The owners claim to use only the catch of the day. Who can carp at such a policy?

✉ **Calle Pestrin 3886**
☎ **041 522 70 24**
🚣 **Arsenale: Nos 1, 41 & 42** 🕐 **Tues-Sat 12.30-2.30pm & 7.30-10.30pm**

Trattoria da Remigio (2, F10) $$
Trattoria
It is not often you find a restaurant that in the early evening can post a sign in the window saying *completo* (full), as though it were a hotel, but this place can. It has a mixed menu, featuring Venetian fish

dishes and some meat options. You'll need to book to be sure of a spot.

✉ **Salizzada dei Greci 3416** ☎ **041 523 00 89**
🚣 **San Zaccaria: Nos 1, 6, 14, 41, 42, 51, 52, 71, 72, 82 & N** 🕐 **Mon 12-3pm, Wed-Sun 12-3pm & 7-11pm** ♿

Trattoria dal Pampo (2, J14) $$
Trattoria
They say *'dal Pampo non c'è scampo'* ('there's no getting away from Pampo') and why would you want to? This is a real locals' place for ombre and cicheti, but you can sit down (inside or out) for a full meal. It is set opposite a charming little park in the quietest end of the city.

✉ **Calle Gen Chinotto 3**
☎ **041 520 84 19**
🚣 **Sant'Elena: Nos 41, 42, 51, 52, 61 & 62**
🕐 **Sat-Thurs 12.30-3pm & 7-10.30pm** ♿

GIUDECCA

Separated by just a wide canal, Giudecca and its handful of eateries are a world away from central Venice.

Ai Tre Scaini (2, K9) $$
Trattoria
In this rambunctious and chaotic trattoria you can settle down with ebullient local families for no-nonsense pasta and seafood dishes. Throaty wine comes from a couple of small barrels set up inside. You can eat in the garden too.

✉ **Calle Michelangelo 53/c** ☎ **041 522 47 90** 🚣 **Zitelle: Nos 41, 42, 82 & N**
🕐 **Mon-Sat 12-2.30pm & 6pm-1am** ♿

All'Altanella (2, K6) $$$
Restaurant
For the average pocket this restaurant is the best deal on the island. Seafood is the speciality and it is an inviting place whatever the season – romantic candle-lit dinners in the winter and alfresco eating beside the canal in summer.

✉ **Calle delle Erbe 268** ☎ **041 522 77 80** 🚣 **Redentore: Nos 41, 42, 82 & N**
🕐 **Wed-Sun 12-3pm & 7-11.30pm** ♿

Harry's Dolci (2, J5) $$$$
Restaurant/Snack Bar
Run by the Hotel Cipriani, this place, with tables by the canal looking across to Dorsoduro, has fantastic desserts (which is the main reason for stopping by). They also do full meals and snacks.

✉ **Fondamenta San Biagio 773** ☎ **041 522 48 44** 🚣 **Palanca: No 41, 42, 82 & N** 🕐 **Apr-Oct: Wed-Mon 12-2.30pm & 7pm-midnight** ♿

WORTH A TRIP

ISLANDS

Al Trono di Attila
(5, A9) $$$
Restaurant
Unless you plan to blow your budget at the Locanda Cipriani, try this place, between the ferry stop and the cathedral. The atmosphere is suitably bucolic and you will want to dine in the charming garden with pergola. Try the *gnocchetti con rucola e scampi* (small gnocchi with rocket and shrimps). Generally it opens for lunch only, unless you book ahead for dinner.
✉ **Fondamenta Borgognoni 7/a, Torcello ☎ 041 73 00 94 🚏 Torcello: No 12 ⏰ Tues-Sun 12-3pm (evenings with reservation only)** ⚹

Locanda Cipriani
(5, A9) $$$$
Restaurant
The Cipriani clan has run this exclusive culinary hideaway since 1946. Ernest Hemingway set down his bags here in 1948 and wrote part of his *Across the River and Into the Trees*. They don't let out rooms in this exquisite rustic retreat anymore,

---

Lapping Up the Views

If you like to look while you eat, you could consider the following:

All'Altanella (p. 87)
Harry's Dolci (p. 87)
Riviera (p. 81)
Trattoria al Ponte (p. 83)

---

but it's an enticing place to splurge on your rumbling tum.
✉ **Piazza Santa Fosca 29, Torcello ☎ 041 73 01 50 🚏 Torcello: No 12 ⏰ Wed-Mon 12-3pm, Sat 12-3pm & 6-11pm**

Osteria dalla Mora
(2, A12) $$
Restaurant
This place looks out over one of the island's canals and is worth considering for lunch or dinner. The *frittura mista*, or mixed fried seafood dish, is a popular request. On nice days tables are set up outside.
✉ **Fondamenta Manin 75, Murano ☎ 041 527 46 06 🚏 Faro: Nos 12, 13, 41, 42, 71, 72 ⏰ Sat-Thurs 12.30-2.30pm & 7pm-11pm** ⚹

Ristorante Galuppi
(5, B9) $$
Restaurant
Voluble waiters greet you here, a perfectly acceptable eatery among several that line the main drag of the festively pastel coloured island (look for the dolls in the window at this one). Abundant serves of medium quality comfort food at reasonable prices make it a safe bet.
✉ **Via B Galuppi 470, Burano ☎ 041 73 00 81 🚏 Burano: No 12 ⏰ Fri-Wed (daily in summer) 12-3pm & 6.30-11pm** ⚹

Trattoria da Scarso
(1, D7) $$
Restaurant
This is a simple trattoria with a pleasant pergola. Set in the tiny old Venetian

settlement of Malamocco, it isn't too heavily frequented by *foresti* (foreigners). The local colour alone makes it an attractive stop.
✉ **Piazzale Malamocco 4, Lido ☎ 041 77 08 34 🚍 No 11 from Lido 🚏 Lido: Nos 1, 6, 14, 17, 51, 52, 61, 62 & 82 ⏰ Tues-Sun 12.30-3pm & 6.30-11.30pm** ⚹

CHIOGGIA

Ostaria da Pupi
(1, D7) $$
Osteria
At Pupi's place a half-dozen tables are huddled together in air-con comfort upstairs, while another five are arranged on the lane in summer. The limited seafood menu is good. Try the *tagliolini al granchio* (thin ribbon pasta with crab) followed by a *griglia-ta mista* (mixed seafood grill).
✉ **Calle Fattorini 255 ☎ 041 40 47 95 🚍 No 11 from Lido 🚏 Lido: Nos 1, 6, 14, 17, 51, 52, 61, 62 & 82 ⏰ Tues-Sun 12-3pm & 7.30-11pm**

Osteria Penzo
(1, D7) $$
Pizzeria/Restaurant
Staff here prepare good local dishes based entirely on the fleet's catch. It is strongly recommended by Venetians who like to make a long lunch day trip of it.
✉ **Calle Larga Bersaglio 526 ☎ 041 40 09 92 🚍 No 11 from Lido 🚏 Lido: Nos 1, 6, 14, 17, 51, 52, 61, 62 & 82 ⏰ Wed-Mon 12.30-2.30pm & 7-11pm**

MESTRE

Da Bepi Venesian
(5, A2) $$
Restaurant

A couple of blocks from the train station, this restaurant has been serving traditional dishes for years. Some say that it is past its prime, but you can still eat well. The place is huge, with four dining areas, and it specialises in fish. Try the *seppie con polenta* (cuttlefish with polenta).

✉ Via Sernaglia 27
☎ 041 92 93 57
🚉 Mestre ⏲ Tues-Sun 12-2.30pm & 7-11pm ♿

Da Luca (5, A2) $$$
Osteria

This place is arguably the best restaurant in Mestre. The owners take you down a unique culinary path which combines Venetian favourites with some good examples of Japanese cooking – it's clearly a fishy affair. The preparation of the dishes is exquisite and the desserts

Sly Grog Shops
Want some no-nonsense plonk for a picnic? Do what the locals do and take an empty mineral water bottle to a wine store for around €2.10 per litre! Here are a few of Nave de Oro's several branches:
- Rio Terrà San Leonardo, Cannaregio 1370 (4, D6)
- Calle dei SS Apostoli, Cannaregio 4657 (3, A12)
- Campo Santa Margherita, Dorsoduro 3664 (3, G3)
- Calle Mondo Nuovo, Castello 5786/b (3, E14)

Damien Simonis

are even better still.
✉ Via Monte Grappa 42
☎ 041 95 71 22
🚉 Mestre ⏲ Mon-Fri 12-2.30pm & 7-11.30pm, Sat 7-11.30pm ♿

Osteria La Pergola
(5, A2) $$
Osteria

As the name suggests, at this osteria you can sit below the vines of the garden pergola and enjoy

some of the better value food in Mestre. How about trying a delicious plate of *pappardelle all'anatra* (a thick pasta with duck)? Venetians swear by this place, which, by the way, does not serve any seafood.
✉ Via Fiume 42
☎ 041 97 49 32
🚉 Mestre ⏲ Mon-Fri 12-2.30pm & 7-11.30pm, Sat 7-11.30pm ♿

ON THE RUN

Pizza by the slice, sandwiches or snacks can be the cheapest way to lunch.

Ai Rusteghi (3, D12) $
Snack Bar

Pop in here for a great range in mini-panini with all sorts of fillings. They also offer good wines. There's nothing better than an ombra or two and a couple of their delicious little panini as a quick lunch-time snack.
✉ Calletta della Bissa, San Marco 5529
☎ 041 523 22 05
🚤 Rialto: Nos 1, 4, 82 & N ⏲ Mon-Sat 9.30am-3pm & 5-8.30pm

Al Vecchio Penasa
(3, G15) $
Bar

Between Riva degli Schiavoni and Campo SS Filippo e Giacomo, this has long been a good spot for its excellent selection of sandwich triangles (*tramezzini*) and snacks at reasonable prices.
✉ Calle delle Rasse, Castello 4587 ☎ 041 523 72 02 🚤 San Zaccaria: Nos 1, 6, 14, 41, 42, 51, 52, 71, 72, 82 & N ⏲ 6.30am-11.30pm ♿

Spizzico (3, F11) $
Pizzeria

For a quick slice of pizza this chain (which is popular across northern Italy) isn't bad. You can take-away or sit down, and if you fancy a burger instead, a **Burger King** is conveniently located on the same premises.
✉ Campo San Luca, San Marco 4475-4476
🚤 Rialto: Nos 1, 4, 82 & N ⏲ 9am-11pm (sometimes closed Sun) ♿

CAFES & SWEETS

You could while away an afternoon indulging in an array of coffees (from espresso to Irish and beyond) in the elegance of what Napoleon once called 'Europe's finest drawing room', St Mark's Square. Or maybe interrupt the sightseeing with a delicious gelato or pastry?

Bar Ae Maravegie
(3, J5) $
Cafe
Enter here all those in need of a sit down, a good sandwich and a coffee, or a stiffer drink. Crowded at lunch time with harried Venetians in search of a quick snack, it is equally handy for exhausted survivors of the Gallerie dell'Accademia.
✉ **Calle del Toletta, Dorsoduro 1185**
☎ **041 523 57 68**
🚤 **Accademia: Nos 1, 3, 4, 82 & N** ⏱ **Mon-Sat 7.30am-8pm**

Bar Pasticceria Ballarin (3, C12) $
Bar/Pastry Shop
Although on the main thoroughfare leading into San Marco, this bar and pastry shop is a solid local enclave. You can stop for a *spritz* (p. 95) or coffee and buy from a reasonable range of cakes and sweets to eat here or takeaway.
✉ **Salizzada San Giovanni Crisostomo,**

Elegant Caffè Quadri

Cannaregio 5794
☎ **041 528 52 73**
🚤 **Rialto: Nos 1, 4, 82 & N** ⏱ **Wed-Mon 8am-8.15pm** 🚻

Caffè Florian
(3, H13) $
Cafe
The plush interior of this, the city's best known cafe, has seen the likes of Lord Byron and Henry James taking breakfast (separately) before they crossed the piazza to Caffè Quadri (see below) for lunch. Venetians started paying exorbitant sums for the pleasure of drinking here in 1720. In the warmer months especially, a quartet plays for customers sitting outside (watch the surcharge on your drinks).
✉ **Piazza San Marco, San Marco 56-59** ☎ **041 520 56 41** 🚤 **Vallaresso & San Marco: Nos 1, 3, 4, 82 & N** ⏱ **Thurs-Tues 9am-10pm**

Caffè Quadri
(3, G13) $
Cafe
Quadri is in much the same league as Florian, and equally steeped in history. Indeed, it actually opened its doors well before its better known competitor, in 1683. They also have a restaurant and frequently present a quartet of their own to compete with Florian in a good natured fashion.
✉ **Piazza San Marco, San Marco 120**
☎ **041 522 21 05**

🚤 **Vallaresso & San Marco: Nos 1, 3, 4, 82 & N** ⏱ **Tues-Sun 9am-midnight**

Gelateria il Doge
(3, G4) $
Gelateria
In among all the cafes, bars and restaurants around this lively section of Dorsoduro is this strategically placed gelateria. The servings are decent and the flavours true!
✉ **Campo Santa Margherita, Dorsoduro 2604** ☎ **041 524 40 49** 🚤 **Ca' Rezzonico: No 1** ⏱ **8am-9pm** 🚻

Gelateria Millefoglie da Tarcisio (3, E5) $
Gelateria
This gelateria, behind the Chiesa di Santa Maria Gloriosa dei Frari, is an excellent ice cream stop, where hordes queue up on hot sunny days. The servings are generous and the ice cream thick and creamy.
✉ **Salizzada San Rocco, San Polo 3033** ☎ **041 524 46 67** 🚤 **San Tomà: Nos 1, 82 & N** ⏱ **8am-10pm** 🚻

Gelateria Nico
(2, H6) $
Gelateria
Head here for the best ice cream in Venice. The locals take their evening stroll along the Zattere while eating their heavily laden cones. You can also just sit down for a juice or coffee.
✉ **Fondamenta Zattere,**

Dorsoduro 922
☎ 041 522 52 93
🚤 Zattere: Nos 51, 52, 61, 62, 82 & N ⏲ Fri-Wed 6.45am-10pm ♿

Lavena (3, G13) **$**
Cafe
Founded in 1750 and a little less renowned than its big brothers (Florian and Quadri; p. 90), Lavena is in the same vein. Wagner was among its more visible customers, but historically gondoliers and *codegas* (stout fellows who lit the way home for people returning at night) also hung out here.
✉ Piazza San Marco, San Marco 133 ☎ 041 522 40 70 🚤 Vallaresso & San Marco: Nos 1, 3, 4, 82 & N
⏲ Apr-Sept: 9am-10pm; Oct-Mar: Wed-Mon 9am-10pm

Pasticceria Da Bonifacio (3, G15) **$**
Pastry Shop
This classic Venetian pastry shop has remained unspoiled by its proximity to St Mark's Square.

Gelateria Nico, the best address for an ice cream stop

Alongside traditional local sweets and pastries you will occasionally encounter other treats sneaked in from surrounding provinces.
✉ Calle degli Albanesi, Castello 4237 ☎ 041 522 75 07 🚤 San Zaccaria: Nos 1, 6, 14, 41, 42, 51, 52, 71, 72, 82 & N ⏲ 7.30am-8.30pm ♿

Pasticceria Marchini (3, H8) **$**
Pastry Shop
You will be spellbound by the offerings in the window of this, one of Venice's most illustrious cake shops. Everything from traditional Venetian pastries and fine chocolates to delicious liquorice is on offer.
✉ Calle del Spezier, San

Marco 2769 ☎ 041 522 91 09 🚤 Santa Maria del Giglio: No 1 ⏲ Wed-Mon 9.30am-8.30pm ♿

Pasticceria Rizzardini (3, D8) **$**
Pastry Shop
Since 1742 this shop has been delivering tempting sweet things to its neighbours. Little seems to have changed since at least the 19th century. There's a tiny display of cakes made to traditional recipes and a bar for local ladies and gents to indulge in a cup of hot chocolate or a little prosecco and some chat.
✉ Campiello dei Meloni, San Polo 1415 ☎ 041 522 38 35 🚤 San Silvestro: No 1 ⏲ 7am-8.45pm

Cafe Culture
- *Espresso* – a small cup of strong black coffee
- *Doppio espresso* – a double espresso
- *Caffè lungo* – watery espresso
- *Caffè americano* – approximation of bland filter coffee
- *Caffellatte* – with milk, a breakfast coffee
- *Cappuccino* – frothy version of a caffellatte, also a breakfast coffee
- *Caffè macchiato* – espresso with a dash of frothy milk
- *Caffè freddo* – a long glass with cold coffee and ice cubes
- *Corretto* – espresso 'corrected' with grappa

entertainment

Venice, its inhabitants and its visitors constitute a theatrical spectacle in themselves. Good thing really because the lagoon city has long shed its 18th century reputation as Europe's premier pleasure dome. Night owls in particular may find the city frustrating. Don't come to Venice for the clubbing!

This is not to say there is *nothing* to do. Thanks in part to the student population and the presence of so many visitors, a pleasing if not abundant array of bars and cafes will keep you occupied until about 2am. Beyond that hour it's slim pickings.

A few cinemas are dotted about the city but movies tend to be dubbed into Italian. Theatre is limited and, naturally, also in Italian. The international language of music offers greater options, ranging from opera to concerts of classical and Baroque music (some border on the cheesy). At a handful of venues you can occasionally catch some jazz or blues.

A string of festivals, traditional and arts, above all the glorious Carnevale in February, fills the Venetian calendar throughout the year. The tourist offices can provide an updated list of events.

Picking up Tickets

Box Office, a nationwide ticketing operation, has two agents in Venice at Gran Canal Viaggi, Ponte dell'Ovo, San Marco 4759-4760 (3, E11; ☎ 041 271 21 11) and the Parole e Musica CD store, Salizzada di San Lio 5673 (3, D13; ☎ 041 523 50 10). You can also book tickets with a credit card by calling Milan on ☎ 02 5 42 71. Ticket One (**e** www.ticketone.it) allows you to book on the Internet.

For some major events you can pick up tickets at Vela (☎ 899 90 90 90, **e** www.velaspa.com) outlets, which are part of the ACTV city transport body. Two Vela points operate by the train station.

For listings of bars, cafes, theatre and cinema, the best source is the monthly bilingual *Venezia News* magazine (€2.05), available at newsstands. *Un Ospite di Venezia*, a free monthly tourist information magazine, available (sometimes) at tourist offices and many hotels, contains less complete listings. You can also check out Ombra.Net (**e** www.ombra.net) and Venice Banana (**e** www.venicebanana.com) Web sites.

Wet your whistle as you soak up the history at Al Bottegon (p. 94).

Damien Simonis

SPECIAL EVENTS

January *Regatta delle Befane* – 6 Jan; the first of the year's more than 100 regattas, this features rowing Venetian-style (voga veneta), which involves various kinds of lagoon boats loosely resembling gondolas, whose crews row standing up

February *Carnevale* – Venetians don spectacular masks and costumes for this week long party in the run up to Ash Wednesday; starting dates for Carnevale in the next couple of years are 25 Feb 2003 and 17 Feb 2004 (see also p. 102)

April *Festa di San Marco* – 25 Apr; on the feast day of the city's patron saint, menfolk give their beloved a bunch of roses

May *Vogalonga* – some 3000 people and boats of all descriptions (powered by human muscle) participate in the 32km 'long row' from San Marco to Burano and back to the Grand Canal
Festa della Sensa – 2nd Sun in May; since AD998 Venice has marked Ascension Day with the Sposalizio del Mar (Marriage to the Sea), a celebration of the city's profitable relationship with the sea (these days the mayor takes on the ducal role); regattas off the Lido
Palio delle Quattro Antiche Repubbliche Marinare – late May-early June; Amalfi, Genoa, Pisa and Venice take turns to host the Historical Regatta of the Four Ancient Maritime Republics, in which four galleons compete; next in Venice in 2003

June *Marciliana* – medieval pageant in Chioggia to commemorate the siege of the city by Genoa in 1380; parades and competition between five *contrade* (town quarters) including rowing and archery
Sagra di San Pietro in Castello – last weekend in June; busy festival with music, drinking and eating at the steps of the church
Venezia Biennale Internazionale d'Arte – June-Oct/Nov; biennial interna- tional exhibition of visual arts held in permanent pavilions near the Giardini Pub- blici and other locations throughout the city

July *Festa del Redentore* – 3rd weekend in Jul; pontoon between Dorsoduro and Chiesa del SS Redentore on Giudecca in thanksgiving celebrations for end of the plague in 1577; fireworks and regattas

September *Regatta Storica* – 1st Sun in Sept; historic gondola race along the Grand Canal and parade of 15th-century-style boats
Mostra del Cinema di Venezia – annual Venice International Film Festival, Italy's version of Cannes, held at the Palazzo del Cinema on the Lido

November *Festa della Madonna della Salute* – 21 Nov; procession on pon- toon across the Grand Canal to the Chiesa di Santa Maria della Salute to give thanks for the city's deliverance from plague in 1630

Damien Simonis

BARS & PUBS

The liveliest areas for bars are in and around the young and bustling Campo Santa Margherita in Dorsoduro (3, G3) and along Fondamenta degli Ormesini (4, B6) and Fondamenta della Misericordia (4, C8) in Cannaregio. More traditional wine bars, or *bacari*, generally close fairly early.

Al Bottegon (Cantina di Vini già Schiavi)
(3, K5) Wander into this fusty old wine bar across from the Chiesa di San Trovaso for a glass of *prosecco* (p. 79) beneath the bar's low-slung rafters and in the wavering light provided by dodgy bulbs. Locals have been doing just that for countless decades. Alternatively, you could just buy a bottle of whatever takes your fancy and take it away.
✉ **Fondamenta Maravegie 992** ☎ **041 523 00 34** 🚤 Zattere: Nos 51, 52, 61, 62, 82 & N ⏰ Mon-Sat to 9pm

Black Jack Bar (3, F11)
Gather around this convivial circular bar in the early evening with locals to sip Bellinis and other classic cocktails while picking away at the colourful array of bar snacks.
✉ **Campo San Luca, San Marco 4267/b** ☎ **041 522 25 18**

🚤 Rialto: Nos 1, 4, 82 & N ⏰ Mon-Sat 7.45am-8.45pm

Brasserie Vecchia Bruxelles (3, E3)
This is a rollicking sort of a place with a genial pub atmosphere, vaguely dressed up as a Belgian beer house, and with a reasonable assortment of ales on offer. The mix is part local student, part foreigner. Karaoke on some nights is a feature that may not appeal to all.
✉ **Salizzada San Pantalon, Santa Croce 81** ☎ **041 71 06 36** 🚤 San Tomà: Nos 1, 82 & N ⏰ 7am-2am

Café Noir (3, F4)
You can start the day with breakfast in here, pop in for some time online on one of the handful of computers or hang out into the night with a mixed crowd of Italian students and foreigners. The place has a laid-back, underground feel about it. A cocktail costs about €3.50.
✉ **Calle San Pantalon, Dorsoduro 3805** ☎ **041 71 09 25** 🚤 San Tomà: Nos 1, 82 & N ⏰ Mon-Sat 7am-2am

Caffè (3, G3)
At the heart of the scene on Campo Santa Margherita is this perennially overcrowded student haunt. Known to locals affectionately as the *caffè rosso* (the 'red cafe') because of the colour of the sign, it draws a happily hip crowd for snacks and drinks.
✉ **Campo Santa Margherita, Dorsoduro 2693** ☎ **041 528 79 98** 🚤 Ca' Rezzonico: No 1 ⏰ Mon-Sat to 1am

Caffè Blue (3, E4)
Although it can get a little quiet on weekday evenings this coolish student bar gets busy at weekends, especially when they put on a little live music (which can range from light jazz to easy pop). Even without, punters end up spilling out onto the street even in the big chill of winter.
✉ **Calle dei Preti, Dorsoduro 3778** ☎ **041 523 72 27** 🚤 San Tomà: Nos 1, 82 & N ⏰ Mon-Sat 8am-2pm & 5pm-2am

Capo Horn (3, F4)
A few steps away from Café Noir (see above), the Capo

Knock a few back at the Black Jack.

Damien Simonis

Horn is decked out as an 18th century sailing vessel. Recently renovated, it is not a bad bar to hang out in for a beer or whisky (of which they have a wide variety). The very happy hour is from 6pm to 8pm, when a *spritz* costs just €0.50.

✉ **Calle San Pantalon, Dorsoduro 3805**
☎ **041 524 21 77**
🚤 **San Tomà: Nos 1, 82 & N** ⏲ **Mon-Sat 8pm-2am**

Cavatappi (3, F13)

A brand new addition to the Venice scene, this modern creamy white bar with halogen lighting has wines from all over Italy. In a rather daring departure for what is in many ways a small town, this place will appeal to all who miss a slightly metropolitan touch. Try cheeses from all over Italy, with a few French and Swiss additions, and if you want to eat, inspect the untraditional menu.

✉ **Campo della Guerra 525, San Marco 3805**
☎ **041 296 02 52**
🚤 **Vallaresso & San Marco: Nos 1, 3, 4, 82 & N** ⏲ **Mon-Sat 9am-midnight (Mon-Sun in summer)**

Da Codroma (3, G2)

Once a good old-fashioned *osteria* (traditional bar/ restaurant) where you could dine on standard Venetian snacks and meals, this place has passed on to become something of a student bar. With its wood panelling, long timber tables and smokily conspiratorial atmosphere, it fulfils the role admirably. You can get snacks and panini to accompany your tipple, and on Sundays they

---

Tippling Town

In a country not noted for heavy drinkers, the Venetians form a category all of their own. Locals can often be seen indulging in alcoholic cardiac stimulation at breakfast time and few skip the chance to have a *prosecco* (light sparking white wine) or two at some point in the day. Early evening is *aperitivo* time, and the favoured beverage is the *spritz* (prosecco, soda water and bitter – Campari, Amaro, Aperol or Select), one of the few things introduced by the Austrians in the 19th century that the Venetians actually grudgingly appreciated. Later on, locals do not disdain a couple of classic Venetian cocktails, such as the Bellini (champagne or prosecco and peach nectar).

---

make a bit of an effort with a variety of *cicheti* (traditional bar snacks).

✉ **Fondamenta Briati, Dorsoduro 2540**
☎ **041 524 67 89**
🚤 **San Basilio: Nos 61, 62, 82 & N** ⏲ **Sun-Fri 8am-midnight**

Devil's Forest (3, E12)

You'll probably ask yourself how they got the old style red telephone box into this imitation UK pub, hidden down a central Venice lane. We did! Oh well, just sidle up to the bar, order a pint of Kilkenny or Harp and watch TV sports in the company of other Anglo interlopers.

✉ **Calle Stagneri, San Marco 5185** ☎ **041 520 00 23** 🚤 **Rialto: Nos 1, 4, 82 & N** ⏲ **Mon-Sat 10am-1pm & 5pm-12.30am**

Harry's Bar (3, J12)

As well as being a noted restaurant (p. 80), Harry's is, of course, first and foremost known as a bar. Everyone who is anyone and passing through Venice usually ends up here sooner or later. Characters as diverse as

---

Orson Welles and Truman Capote have sipped on a cocktail or two at Harry's. White-jacketed waiters rush about the small simple tables taking orders for Bellinis (a mere €12) and other grand tipples.

✉ **Calle Vallaresso, San Marco 1323**
☎ **041 528 57 77**
🚤 **Vallaresso & San Marco: Nos 1, 3, 4, 82 & N** ⏲ **12-11pm**

Il Muro (3, F10)

When things around this part of town start to look grim, people converge on this nameless bar, universally known as Il Muro (The Wall). Late on a Friday or Saturday night it's a lively joint for a drink – and the only seriously decent option in the San Marco area.

✉ **Calle San Antonio, San Marco 4118**
☎ **041 520 52 05**
🚤 **Vallaresso & San Marco: Nos 1, 3, 4, 82 & N** ⏲ **7pm-2am**

La Fondamenta

(4, C8) This is a cheap and cheerful restaurant that from a culinary point

of view is nothing special, but locals turn up to use its services as a bar, spilling out onto the *fondamenta* well into the summer nights. It's quiet in winter.
✉ **Fondamenta della Misericordia, Cannaregio 2578** ☎ **041 71 73 15** 🚣 **Madonna dell'Orto: Nos 41, 42, 51 & 52** ⏰ **Wed-Mon 11am-3pm & 5pm-2am**

Le Bistrot de Venise
(3, F12) As much restaurant as bar, this bistrot is an elegant setting for a little wine tasting accompanied by nibbles, particularly Italian and French cheeses. An eclectic spot, you may well run into an evening of jazz or poetry readings.
✉ **Calle dei Fabbri, San Marco 4685** ☎ **041 523 66 51** e **www.bistrotdevenise .com** 🚣 **Rialto: Nos 1, 4, 82 & N** ⏰ **10-1am**

Margaret Duchamp
(3, G4) Across the square from the above mentioned Caffè (p. 94), the Margaret Duchamp is set at a strategic angle and is perennially popular with a mixed crowd of locals, students and blow-ins. It's the perfect spot for seeing and being seen.
✉ **Campo Santa**

Margherita, Dorsoduro 3019 ☎ **041 528 62 55** 🚣 **Ca' Rezzonico: No 1** ⏰ **noon-2am**

Martini Scala (3, H10) Walk down the stairs here into another era. The tinkling of the piano and the clinking of ice cubes in your tumbler will be enough to make you wonder where you left your cigars. It is all a little cheesy and very pricey, but then the options aren't bountiful (especially this late at night), are they?
✉ **Calle della Veste, San Marco 1501** ☎ **041 522 41 21** 🚣 **Santa Maria del Giglio: No 1** ⏰ **Wed-Mon 9pm-3.30am**

Osteria agli Ormesini
(4, B7) Oodles of wine and 120 types of bottled beer in one knockabout little place? Perhaps you should get along to this osteria. It's something of a student haunt for those who like that kind of gruff service and no-nonsense ambience.
✉ **Fondamenta degli Ormesini, Cannaregio 2710** ☎ **041 71 38 34** 🚣 **Madonna dell'Orto: Nos 41, 42, 51 & 52** ⏰ **Mon-Sat to 2am**

Round Midnight
(3, H4) After you've soaked up the atmosphere on Campo Santa Margherita, head to this drinking den on a nearby back canal. You can sip on all sorts of cocktails, get a snack and even have a bit of a dance. The music tends towards acid jazz and Latin.
✉ **Fondamenta dei Squero, Dorsoduro 3102** ☎ **041 523 20 56** 🚣 **Ca' Rezzonico: No 1** ⏰ **Sept-May: Mon-Sat 7pm-4am**

Taverna da Baffo
(3, D6) Named after Casanova's licentious poet pal Giorgio Baffo and lined with his rhymes in praise of 'the round arse' and other zones of the female anatomy, this bar has a young chirpy feel. In summer the tables outside are an especially pleasant spot to sip on a spritz or two.
✉ **Campiello Sant' Agostin, Dorsoduro 2346** ☎ **041 520 88 62** 🚣 **San Tomà: Nos 1, 82 & N** ⏰ **Mon-Sat 7am-2am**

Torino@Notte (3, F11) During the day this cafe-bar is a fairly mundane, if busy, locale where you can drop in for a snack, beer or coffee. It makes an unlikely setting for its nocturnal transformation, as a young student set settles in for mixed drinks, music and occasionally even a live act.
✉ **Campo San Luca, San Marco 459** ☎ **041 522 39 14** 🚣 **Rialto: Nos 1, 4, 82 & N** ⏰ **Tues-Sat 10pm-1am**

Vino Vino (3, H10)
See p. 80.

Shaken, not Stirred

Truman Capote called a good Martini a Silver Bullet. What's in it? Quality gin and a drop of Martini Dry. Of course the amount of the latter varies according to taste: for a strong, dry Martini, 'rinse' the glass with Martini and then pour in freezing gin. Hemingway, who set part of his book *Across the River and into the Trees* at Harry's, had his own recipe: pour freezing cold gin into a glass dipped in ice and sit it next to a bottle of Martini for a moment, then drink!

DANCE CLUBS

Clubbing in Venice is poor. The Lido di Jesolo sees some action in summer – keep an eye on *Venezia News* (see p. 92) for details.

Casanova (4, E3)
A quick stumble from the train station, this is it, about the only place in Venice that can vaguely call itself a disco (more than it can a club). Each night has its own musical theme, from rock revival on Thursday to Latin on Friday and house on Saturday.
✉ **Lista di Spagna, Cannaregio 158/a** ☎ **041 275 01 99, 339 41 77 27**
e **www.casanova.it**
🚊 **Ferrovia: Nos 1, 3, 4, 41, 42, 51, 52, 71, 72, 82 & N** ⏱ **Tues & Thurs-Sat 6pm-4am** ⑤ **€6.20 (inc 1st drink)**

Magic Bus (5, A2)
Big and popular, Magic Bus administers a diet of 90s rock and occasionally stages live concerts.
✉ **Via delle Industrie**

1118, Marcon, Mestre
☎ **041 59 52 15**
🚊 **Mestre, then taxi**
⏱ **Fri-Sat 11pm-5am**
⑤ **€10.35**

Metrò (5, A2)
In the centre of Mestre, you can sip cocktails and listen to good music here. The latter depends on the day and ranges from 80s to Latin to house. You might want to skip karaoke night on Tuesday.
✉ **Via Einaudi 19, Mestre** ☎ **041 95 92 62** 🚊 **Mestre, then taxi**
⏱ **Mon-Sat 10pm-4am**
⑤ **varies**

Piccolo Mondo (3, J6)
This teeny little disco and bar is slightly on the slimy side, but perfectly all right in its own wide-lapel fashion. It attracts a 30s plus

crowd and makes you feel like you have been catapulted into a smoke filled 70s movie.
✉ **Calle Corfu, Dorsoduro 1506** ☎ **041 520 03 71** 🚊 **Accademia: Nos 1, 3, 4, 82 & N**
⏱ **Tues-Sun to 4am**

The Zoo (5, A6)
Another favourite in the Mestre area, this venue, out in Tessera, is virtually opposite Marco Polo airport. In four dance spaces you can weave from house to Latin rhythms to mainstream international and Italian pop.
✉ **Via Ca' Zorzi 2, Mestre, Tessera**
☎ **348 989 7017**
🚊 **Mestre, then taxi**
⏱ **Fri & Sat 11pm-4am**
⑤ **up to €13**

ROCK, JAZZ & BLUES

Live-music performances are sporadic in Venice – check what's on before you head off anywhere. Watch the local press for annual events in Jesolo (1, C8) and Marghera (5, C3). A Contemporary Music Festival is held annually in October at the Teatro Goldoni (p. 98).

Musical Munch

If you want chow with your tunes or salad with your ballads, try one of these venues for dinner:

- Arca (p. 81)
- Cantina Vecia Carbonera (p. 84)
- Paradiso Perduto (p. 85)

Pizzeria Jazz Club 900
(3, C9) Decked out in early 20th century fashion, this spot, hidden away on a tiny square, is a north point for jazz musicians in Venice. Wednesdays is a good bet for performances and if you get peckish they serve decent pizza.
✉ **Campiello Sansoni, San Polo 900** ☎ **041 522 65 65** 🚊 **Rialto: Nos 1, 4, 82 & N** ⏱ **Tues-Sun 11.30am-4pm & 7pm-2am**

Vapore (5, B2)
About the best place for a consistent programme of jazz, blues and other music, Vapore is in rather dispiriting Marghera, on the mainland. The club occasionally attracts good foreign acts as well as more local talent.
✉ **Via Fratelli Bandiera 8, Marghera**
☎ **041 93 07 96**
🚊 **Mestre, then taxi**
⏱ **varies** ⑤ **varies**

OPERA, THEATRE & DANCE

The star of Venetian theatre and opera was for centuries the Teatro La Fenice, Campo San Fantin, San Marco 1970 (3, H9), a sad hulk since fire destroyed it in 1996. Performances are now held at a couple of alternative venues, tickets for which are available from those theatres (see below), Vela outlets, the Internet and the Cassa di Risparmio di Venezia bank, Campo San Luca (3, F11; ☎ 041 521 01 61; Mon-Fri 8.30am-1.30pm).

Apart from those listed below, several smaller theatres, some of them fairly lean and experimental, are scattered about Venice, Mestre and the hinterland.

PalaFenice (2, E1)
In the wake of the fire of 1996, a temporary alternative location for La Fenice performances was set up on Tronchetto island within a series of big-top-style tents. They're still there today. It's hardly a glamorous replacement and is also stretched to capacity.
✉ **Isola del Tronchetto**
☎ **041 78 65 01**
e **www.teatrolafenice .it** 🚊 Tronchetto: Nos 3, 4, 71, 72, 82 & N ⑤ up to €35

Teatro Goldoni
(3, E11) This place is named after the city's greatest playwright, and is, unsurprisingly, the main theatre in the centre of town. It's not unusual for Goldoni's plays to be

Goldoni's greenroom

performed here.
✉ **Calle Teatro Goldoni, San Marco 4650/b** ☎ **041 520 75 83, 041 240 20 14 (box office)** **e** **www.teatro goldonive.it** 🚊 Rialto: Nos 1, 4, 82 & N ⑤ up to €30 ♿

Teatro Malibran
(3, C13) After years of work on its restoration,

this exquisite 17th century theatre was reopened in 2001. It serves mainly as an adjunct to the PalaFenice, sharing the programme burden.
✉ **Calle del Teatro, San Marco 5870**
☎ **041 78 65 20**
e **www.teatrolafenice .it** 🚊 Rialto: Nos 1, 4, 82 & N ⑤ up to €35

Teatro Toniolo (5, A2)
A busy theatre in the centre of Mestre, Teatro Toniolo puts on eclectic programmes ranging from Shakespeare to local drama, even occasionally in dialect.
✉ **Piazzetta C Battisti 1, Mestre** ☎ **041 97 16 66** **e** **www.comune .venezia.it/teatrotoniolo** 🚊 Mestre, then taxi ⑤ up to €20 ♿

Teatro Malibran, supposedly built on the site of Marco Polo's family abode.

BAROQUE PERFORMANCES

Musical ensembles dressed in billowing 18th century costume regularly perform concerts of Baroque and light classical music from about April to September. Clearly these shows are aimed at tourists and can be cheesy, but the musical quality is not necessarily bad. The two standard Venetians Vivaldi and Albinoni figure largely in the repertoires of these groups.

Popular venues, other than those mentioned below, include the **Chiesa di San Bartolomeo** (3, D11) and the **Chiesa delle Zitelle** (2, J9). Venues tend to change lot, as do the various groups, so look out for fliers to see what's on offer. Alternatively, information and tickets for the following and other similar performances are available from Agenzia Kele & Teo, Ponte dei Baratteri, San Marco (3, F12; ☎ 041 520 87 22). Many hotels can also help. Expect to pay €20.70-31/person for most performances.

Concerti della Venezia Musica

Divided into several different ensembles, such as the five member Putte di Vivaldi (Vivaldi's Girls) and the grander I Virtuosi dell'Ensemble, this gang performs a range of Venetian Baroque music, usually at the church where Vivaldi himself often worked, the Chiesa della Pietà, aka the Chiesa di Vivaldi, Riva degli Schiavoni, Castello 4149 (2, G10).
☎ 041 523 10 96
e www.vivaldi.it

Damien Simonis

Check out Vivaldi's Girls at the Chiesa della Pietà.

Concerto in Gondola

This waterborne version of Venetian Baroque comprises a fleet of gondolas that float between Ponte di Rialto and Ponte dell'Accademia accompanied by a barge-like vehicle on which a gaggle of musicians play, dressed in full 18th century garb. They offer a mixed selection of light classical and opera (Puccini, Mozart and the usual suspects).
☎ 041 521 02 94
e www.concertin gondola.com
🚣 San Tomà: Nos 1, 82 & N ⑤ €43.90

I Musici Veneziani

This group, resplendent in 18th century costume, offers a fairly broad repertoire that sometimes ventures into opera and can range from morsels of Mozart to bits of Offenbach. At the time of writing they performed mainly at the Scuola Grande di San Teodoro, Campo San Salvador, San Marco 4811 (3, E11).
☎ 041 521 02 94
e www.imusicivenezi ani.com

Orchestra di Venezia

Decidedly more Venetian in its approach, sticking with Vivaldi, Albinoni and co, this group includes dance in its programme. The orchestra happily switches from classical to traditional Venetian ballads. They generally perform at the Scuola Grande di San Giovanni Evangelista, Campiello San Giovanni, Santa Croce 2454 (3, D5).
☎ 041 522 81 25
e www.orchestra .venezia.it

CINEMAS

The cinema scene is limited in Venice and you will be unlikely to see anything in English. In July and August a big screen is erected in Campo San Polo, which makes for one of the more magical settings for outdoor cinema. It costs around €6 to go to the movies.

Cinema Accademia d'Essai (3, J6)

A fusty old place containing a couple of screens offering indifferent picture quality, this does have the merit of offering some quite decent flicks – rigorously dubbed into Italian however.

✉ **Calle Corfu, Dorsoduro 1018** ☎ **041 528 77 06**

🚊 **Accademia: Nos 1, 3, 4, 82 & N** ⊘ **Wed-Mon 2 or 3 sessions (around 4pm, 6pm and 9.15pm)** ♿

Cinema Giorgione Movie d'Essai (3, A12)

The Giorgione is a comparatively modern cinema complex where they present a reasonable range of decent movies but, again, generally dubbed into Italian.

✉ **Rio Terrà Franceschi, Cannaregio 4612** ☎ **041 522 62 98**

🚊 **Fondamente Nuove: Nos 12, 13, 41, 42, 51 & 52** ⊘ **2 or 3 sessions (around 4pm, 6pm & 9.15pm)** ♿

CASINOS

Some people find Venice a haunting and melancholy place. No doubt those who have lost at the gaming tables of the casino are among them. It's a dangerous and moveable feast, with an historic location on the Grand Canal and a brand spanking new complex on the mainland (the summer casino on the Lido is no more).

Casinò Municipale di Venezia (4, E7)

Housed in the Renaissance Palazzo Vendramin-Calergi, where the composer Richard Wagner passed on in 1883, the gambler will find all of his or her old favourites, from slot machines to roulette. It is a rather formal affair with jacket and tie required (no doubt the latter can come off as the heat rises).

✉ **Palazzo Vendramin-Calergi, Cannaregio 2040** ☎ **041 529 71 11** 🌐 **www.casinovenezia.it**

🚊 **San Marcuola: Nos 1, 82 & N** ⊘ **Oct-May: 3pm-3am** 💲 **€2.60 (to gaming rooms)**

Venice Casino (1, B7)

Opened to the public in 2001, this is Italy's premier mainland gambling house. It is a bigger, more modern and a more casual affair than its staid senior partner in Venice. If gambling is more important to you than the historical setting in which you place your bets, head here.

✉ **Ca' Noghera, Via Triestina 222, Tessera** ☎ **041 529 71 11** 🌐 **www.casinovenezia .it** 🚌 **free hrly shuttle from Piazzale Roma** ⊘ **Sun-Fri 11-4.45am, Sat 11-6am** 💲 **Sun-Thurs €2.60; Fri-Sat €5.20**

Damien Simonis

Place your bets and cross your fingers!

SPECTATOR SPORTS

Football

Like anywhere else in Italy, *il calcio* reigns supreme in the hearts and minds of many a Venetian. The *arancioneroverde* (orange, black and greens) are a middling team rarely touched by the pleasure of competition victory. Indeed, they suffered the indignity of going down to the 2nd division (Serie B) in 2000, but managed to re-emerge in the top division (Serie A) for the 2001-02 season.

The team plays at the Stadio Penzo, on Isola Sant'Elena (p. 49), at the far eastern end of the lagoon city. The uniqueness of the team's home town makes for some interesting logistics when the side plays at home. Special ferry services are laid on between Tronchetto car park and Sant' Elena – normally a quiet little place with hardly a soul to disturb the leafy peace. All buses arriving in Venice on a match day are diverted first to Tronchetto to disgorge their loads of fans before reaching Piazzale Roma.

You can purchase tickets from branches of Banca Antoniana Popolare Veneta, Vela outlets and at the stadium. An average seat costs around €18. The bank used as a ticket outlet can change from year to year, so ask at the tourist office or call Venezia Calcio (☎ 041 95 81 00) to find out which one to head for. Getting tickets on match days is rarely a problem.

No sitting down on the job!

Rowing

The *voga veneta*, or Venetian rowing (in all its forms), is not just for gondoliers. You will see people standing up in various odd-looking boats and punts and pushing themselves about the lagoon. Numerous regattas are held throughout the year (see p. 93).

Gay & Lesbian Venice
Virtually nothing is done to cater specifically for gays and lesbians in Venice. The nearest gay information centre is more than discreetly located on the mainland: ArciGay Dedalo, Via Costa 38/a, Mestre (5, A2; ☎ 041 753 84 15). They will probably tell you to head for clubs in far away Padua.

Rites of Spring

Venetians have been celebrating the approach of spring with their Carnevale (Carnival) at least since the 15th century. In those days private clubs organised masked balls, and popular entertainment included such fun as bull-baiting and firing live dogs from cannons! By the 18th century Venice was home to hedonism and the licentious goings-on of Carnevale lasted for two months.

Things quietened down after the city's fall to Napoleon in 1797 and Carnevale later died when Mussolini banned the wearing of masks. Revived in 1979, it has become the world's best known Baroque fancy dress party, as extravagant as Rio's Carnival is riotous.

The festivities begin on a Friday afternoon (dates move around a bit – see p. 93) with La Festa delle Marie, a procession through the city. This is a precursor to the official opening on Saturday, when a traditional masked procession leaves St Mark's Square around 4pm and circulates through the streets. The following day there are jousts and other mock military tournaments.

The following Thursday is Giovedì Grasso, a festival that has always been a part of Venice's celebration of Carnevale. Friday afternoon's highlight is the Gran Ballo delle Maschere (Grand Masked Ball) in St Mark's Square. Anyone with proper costume and mask who is able to dance the quadrilles and other steps of a few centuries ago may join in.

Saturday and Sunday are given over to musical and theatrical performances in St Mark's Square. Also, on the Sunday, a beautiful procession of decorated boats and gondolas bearing masked passengers wends its way serenely down the Grand Canal.

The event winds up with a parade of the Re del Carnevale (Carnival King) and the one-time guilds of the city.

During the course of the festivities plenty goes on outside the main events – street performers fill the main thoroughfares and squares. Campo San Polo (3, D7) is often given over to children's theatre, jugglers and the like for the little 'uns. For a feel of how Carnevale was centuries ago, head for the Vecio Carnevale in Via G Garibaldi (2, H12).

The Grand Canal itself is the centre of events. Throughout the Carnevale period it is kept lit by torch light during the evenings.

The fantastic festivities of Carnevale are sure to put a smile on your face.

Damien Simonis

places to stay

Venice lives to a large extent from tourism so it is no surprise that this compact city is jam-packed with hundreds of hotels. They range from simple family-run establishments to the extravagantly luxurious honey pots that draw celebs. Quality varies enormously and price does not always guarantee it. It is possible to find romantic rooms with ceiling frescoes in centuries-old *palazzi* (squares) for much less than often more clinical rooms in some of the grander sounding places.

Hotels around St Mark's Square (Piazza San Marco) clearly feel obliged to charge extraordinary sums, especially when they look out over the Grand Canal or Bacino di San Marco. A bevy of budget hotels, convenient but frequently not great value, is cluttered around Lista di Spagna that leads from the train station towards the centre.

Increasingly, quality budget digs, along with an array of mid-range and some grander options, are spread farther away from these standard poles of attention, in quieter corners of districts such as Dorsoduro, Santa Croce and Cannaregio. The occasional fine deal still lurks in the heart of the San Marco district and neighbouring Castello.

Hotels go by other names too. The Italian *albergo* means hotel, while a *locanda* or *pensione* indicates a more modest family-run establishment. However, increasingly the terms are blurred.

Room Rates

The categories indicate the cost per night of a standard double room in high season.

Deluxe	from €400
Top End	€201-399
Mid-Range	€100-200
Budget	under €100

Live in luxury at the Londra Palace (p. 104).

Venice is a cramped city where space is at a premium. Rooms are often small, even at pricey places. In most upper-level hotels you can expect a standard array of amenities: phone, TV (often satellite), minibar, safe, air-conditioning, en suite bathroom with hairdryer, and 24 hour service. Only a chosen few can offer extras such as pools. Mid-range places tend to offer only the phone, TV and air-conditioning. Rooms in many budget locales have only a washbasin, with a shared bathroom in the corridor.

Single travellers frequently get stung, as many hotels offer only double rooms at slightly reduced rates to loners.

DELUXE

Bauer (3, J11)

If you don't mind the 1949 Soviet style entrance, the canalside neo-Gothic frontage of this historic *palazzo* (palace) is sufficiently chic. The views across the Grand Canal are hard to beat. Elegant 2nd floor rooms drip Carrara marble and Murano glass.
✉ Campo San Moisè, San Marco 1459 ☎ 041 520 70 22; fax 041 520 75 57 e info@bauer venezia.it; www.bauer venezia.it 🛥 Vallaresso & San Marco: Nos 1, 3, 4, 82 & N ✕ De Pisis & bar

Cipriani (2, J9)

Set in the one time villa of the Mocenigo noble family and surrounded by lavish grounds, the Cipriani has unbeatable views across to San Marco, and an elite feel. You can dine excellently in the hotel restaurant and a private launch runs between the hotel and San Marco.
✉ Giudecca 10 ☎ 041 520 77 44; fax 041 520 39 30 e info@hotelcipriani.it; www.hotelcipriani.it 🛥 Zitelle: Nos 41, 42,

82 & N ✕ Cipriani, Cip's Club Terrace & bars

Palatial Danieli

Danieli (3, G15)

Most of the rooms in this Venetian classic overlook the water. It opened as a hotel in 1822 in the 14th century Palazzo Dandolo. Dining in the rooftop restaurant is a feast for the eyes as well as the palate.
✉ Riva degli Schiavoni, Castello 4196 ☎ 041 522 64 80; fax 041 520 02 08 e res072.danieli@star woodhotels.com; www .starwood.com/luxury 🛥 San Zaccaria: Nos 1, 6, 14, 41, 42, 51, 52, 71, 72, 82 & N ✕ La Terrazza & bars

Excelsior (5, F7)

A fanciful Moorish style property, the Excelsior has long been the top address on the Lido. Many of the luxurious rooms look out to sea or across the lagoon to Venice. There are outdoor and heated pools if the beach seems too far away!
✉ Lungomare Guglielmo Marconi 41, Lido ☎ 041 526 02 01; fax 041 526 72 76 e www .starwood.com/westin 🛥 Lido: Nos 1, 6, 14, 51, 52, 61, 62 & 82 ✕ Tropicana & bars

Gritti Palace (3, J9)

If you stay at the Gritti, one of the most famous hotels in Venice, you'll be mixing with celebs and royalty. A good portion of Hemingway's *Across the River and Into the Trees* is set here.
✉ Campo Traghetto 2467 ☎ 041 79 46 11; fax 041 520 09 42 e www.starwood .com/luxury 🛥 Santa Maria del Giglio: No 1 ✕ Club del Doge & Bar Longhi

Londra Palace

(2, G10) Most of the rooms at this four star property have views over the water. Completely renovated in 1998, the rooms feature 19th century furniture, Jacuzzis and marble bathrooms.
✉ Riva degli Schiavoni, Castello 4171 ☎ 041 520 05 33; fax 041 522 50 32 e info@hotelondra.it; www.hotelondra.it 🛥 San Zaccaria: Nos 1, 6, 14, 41, 42, 51, 52, 71, 72, 82 & N ✕ Do Leoni & wine bar

---

Book Ahead

If you arrive in Venice without a booking, you can try for a late reservation (for a small fee of €0.50-2) at the Associazione Veneziana Albergatori. The main office is at Stazione di Santa Lucia (3, B1; ☎ 041 71 52 88; 8am-10pm), and there are two in Piazzale Roma (2, F4), and one each at the Tronchetto car park (2, D1) and the airport (5, A7). They also have 'last-minute' booking numbers: ☎ 800 84 30 06 (from within Italy, toll free) or ☎ 041 522 22 64 (from abroad).

Damien Simons

TOP END

Ca' Pisani Hotel

(3, K6) Named after a 14th century Venetian hero, this centuries-old building houses a curious departure in Venice – a self-conscious design hotel, filled with 1930s and 40s furnishings and items especially made for the hotel. The rooms, some with exposed beam ceilings, are well equipped and full of pleasing decorative touches.

✉ Rio Terrà Antonio Foscarini, Dorsoduro 979a ☎ 041 277 14 78; fax 041 277 10 61 ℮ info@capisanihotel .it; www.capisanihotel .it ⚓ Accademia: Nos 1, 3, 4, 82 & N ✕ La Rivista

Grand Hotel Des Bains

(5, F8) This is the top address for Thomas Mann fans. Take a room at the tail end of the season to enjoy the full melancholy effect. Mann's character Aschenbach probably wasn't into the sporty activities on offer here, which range from tennis to horse riding. The hotel is closed from late October to April.

✉ Lungomare Guglielmo Marconi 17, Lido ☎ 041 526 59 21; fax 041 526 01 13 ℮ www.starwood .com/sheraton ⚓ Lido: Nos 1, 6, 14, 51, 52, 61, 62 & 82 ✕ Liberty & bars

Grand Hotel Palazzo dei Dogi

(4, A8) Once an embassy, this haughty hotel stands in splendid isolation in the northwest of the city.

Apartment Rental

An alternative to hotels is to rent an apartment. At ℮ www.wotspot.com/venice you can find flats in the Santa Croce area for as little as €60/day. Euroflats (℮ www.ccrsrl.com) has flats sleeping up to four from €700/week. For luxury apartments try Guest in Italy (℮ www.guestinitaly.com) or Venetian Apartments (℮ www.venicerentals.com). You could pay €2000/week sleeping up to six.

The airy rooms are well appointed in 18th century style and the presidential suite enjoys magnificent views out to the island of Murano. Other rooms face the tranquil private gardens.

✉ Fondamenta Madonna dell'Orto, Cannaregio 3500 ☎ 041 220 81 11; fax 041 72 22 78 ℮ reception@ deidogi.boscolo.com; www.boscolohotels .com/dogi ⚓ Madonna dell'Orto: Nos 41, 42, 51 & 52 ✕

Hotel Giorgione

(3, A12) In this welcoming hotel you will find comfortable, although in some cases rather small, rooms mostly in a 15th century mansion (part of the building is modern). A couple of the best top-floor rooms have little terraces. It is possible to take breakfast in the courtyard.

✉ Calle Larga dei Proverbi, Cannaregio 4587 ☎ 041 522 58 10; fax 041 523 90 92 ℮ giorgione@ hotelgiorgione.com; www.hotelgiorgione .com ⚓ Fondamente Nuove: Nos 1, 2, 13, 41, 42, 51 & 52 ✕

Hotel San Cassiano

(3, B9) The 14th century Ca' Favretto houses a selection of rooms: the better ones are high-ceilinged doubles overlooking the Grand Canal. The building is a wonderful old pile, with stone doorways along the staircases. Grab a table on the balcony for breakfast on the canal.

✉ Calle della Rosa, Santa Croce 2232 ☎ 041 524 17 68; fax 041 72 10 33 ℮ info@sancassiano.it; www.sancassiano.it ⚓ San Stae: Nos 1 & N ✕ Vecio Fritolin (p. 83)

Hotel Scandinavia

(3, E15) This 15th century converted mansion (the foundations go back to the 11th century) is not a bad choice. The heavy timber beams and 18th-century furnishings give the rooms a cosy touch – the best ones look on to the square. Rates vary considerably and can drop by two thirds in slow periods.

✉ Campo Santa Maria Formosa, Castello 5240 ☎ 041 522 35 07; fax 041 523 52 32 ℮ info@scandinavia hotel.com; www.scan dinaviahotel.com

🚹 San Zaccaria: Nos 1, 6, 14, 41, 42, 51, 52, 71, 72, 82 & N ✕ Osteria al Mascaron (p. 86)

Hotel Tre Archi

(4, A1) The Tre Archi, an attractive hotel of 24 rooms set well away from the tourist rush, opened in mid-2001. The place is furnished in classical Venetian style. Some rooms (two with a small terrace) look over the Canale di Cannaregio, while others give on to the internal garden, where you can take breakfast in summer.

✉ Fondamenta di Cannaregio, Cannaregio 923 ☎/fax 041 524 43 56 📧 info@hotel trearchi.com; www .hoteltrearchi.com
🚹 Tre Archi: Nos 41, 42, 51 & 52

Villa Mabapa

(5, E8) This pleasant hideaway, a grand old residence in a building dating from the 1930s with a couple of annexes, is frequently booked out in summer and for the cinema festival in September. Rooms have elegant period furniture. You can dine in the garden.

✉ Riviera San Nicolò 16 ☎ 041 526 05 90; fax 041 526 94 41 📧 info@ villamabapa.com; www.villamabapa.com
🚹 Lido: Nos 1, 6, 14, 17, 51, 52, 61, 62 & 82 ✕ Ristorante Villa Mapaba

MID-RANGE

Al Gambero (3, F12)

This hotel is in a great location off St Mark's Square. Clean, comfortable rooms come with TV, phone, and a hairdryer in the bathroom.

✉ Calle dei Fabbri, San Marco 4687 ☎ 041 522 43 84; fax 041 520 04 31 📧 hotelgambero@tin.it
🚹 Rialto: Nos 1, 4, 82 & N ✕

Albergo agli Alboretti (3, K6)

This is a charming hotel that almost feels like an inviting mountain chalet when you step inside. In its category, it is one of Venice's better choices. The management is friendly and the rooms tastefully arranged. The restaurant is also of a high standard.

✉ Rio Terrà Antonio Foscarini, Dorsoduro 884 ☎ 041 523 00 58; fax 041 521 01 58 📧 alborett@gpnet.it
🚹 Accademia: No 1, 3, 4, 82 & N ✕

Albergo al Nuovo Teson (2, G11)

Secreted away on a square with real local flavour, this hotel is a good option. Here you feel you have moved away from the glitz and tourist crush into a grittier side of Venice. There's nothing gritty about the elegantly furnished rooms, which are equipped with shower, TV and phone.

✉ Calle della Pescaria, Castello 3980 ☎/fax 041 520 55 55
🚹 Arsenale: Nos 1, 41 & 42 ✕ Al Covo (p. 86)

Albergo Paganelli

(2, G10) This place is a good deal if you get one of the three waterfront rooms. It has been a hotel since the mid-19th century. The most expensive rooms have views over the lagoon. Others, including some without their own bathroom, can almost halve in price.

✉ Riva degli Schiavoni, Castello 4182 ☎ 041 522 43 24; fax 041 523 92 67 📧 hotelpag@tin.it; www.hotelpaganelli .com 🚹 San Zaccaria: Nos 1, 6, 14, 41, 42, 51, 52, 71, 72, 82 & N
✕ Trattoria da Remigio (p. 87)

Hotel Abbazia (4, E2)

Beyond the reception you pass through the one time refectory of this former abbey. Tunnel-like corridors on the ground floor lead to rooms of varying sizes, but all have big comfortable beds and are well kept. Some look on to the internal courtyard. On the upper floors are some charming suites. Decor tends to be conservative classic, with variations in colour theme. Out of season, prices drop considerably.

✉ Calle Priuli detta dei Cavalletti, Cannaregio 68 ☎ 041 71 73 33; fax 041 71 79 49 📧 info@abbaziahotel .com; www.abbaziahotel .com 🚹 Ferrovia: Nos 1, 3, 4, 41, 42, 51, 52, 71, 72, 82 & N

Hotel alla Salute da Cici (2, H7)

This is a comfortable hotel in a well kept old Venetian house. Some rooms look on to the canal and the owners also have a couple of cheaper singles without own bathroom.

✉ Fondamenta Ca' Balà,

Dorsoduro 222
☎ 041 523 54 04; fax
041 522 22 71
e hotel.salute.dacici@
iol.it 🚊 Salute: No 1

Hotel Messner (2, H7)
The Messner is tucked away
on a tiny street and has the
feel of a rambling private
home. It was fairly recently
overhauled and boasts an
inviting bar and courtyard.
The rooms are cosy and
kept spotlessly clean.
✉ **Rio Terrà del
Spezier, Dorsoduro 216**
☎ 041 522 74 43;
fax 041 522 72 66
e messner@doge.it
🚊 Salute: No 1 ✗

La Calcina (2, H6)
John Ruskin wrote *The
Stones of Venice* in this little hotel, which has a
smidgin of garden attached.
The immaculate rooms are
sober but charming with
small terraces or views. You
can dine canalside.
✉ **Fondamenta Zattere
ai Gesuati, Dorsoduro
780** ☎ 041 520 64 66;
fax 041 522 70 45
e info@lacalcina.com;
www.lacalcina.com
🚊 Zattere: Nos 51, 52,
61, 62, 82 & N ✗

La Residenza (2, G11)
If you don't need watery
views, head to this delightful 15th century mansion,
also known as Palazzo
Gritti-Badoer. The sumptuous upstairs hall makes an
impression with its cande-
labras and elaborate decor.
The rooms are more
restrained, but fine value.
✉ **Campo Bandiera e
Moro, Castello 3608**
☎ 041 528 53 15;
fax 041 523 88 59
e info@venicela
residenza.com;

Damien Simonis

Charming La Calcina

www.venicelaresidenza
.com 🚊 San Zaccaria:
Nos 1, 6, 14, 41, 42, 51,
52, 71, 72, 82 & N
✗ Al Covo (p. 86)

Locanda Leon Bianco
(3, B11) Up from an air-
less courtyard you chance
upon this little centuries-
old jewel. The best three
rooms (of eight) look right
on to the Grand Canal.
The undulating floors and
heavy timber doors with
their original locks lend
the rooms real charm.
✉ **Campiello Leon
Bianco, Cannaregio
5629** ☎ 041 523 35 72;
fax 041 241 63 92
e info@leonbianco.it;
www.leonbianco.it
🚊 Ca' d'Oro: Nos 1 & N

Locanda Remedio
(3, F14) This inn, in a
tranquil courtyard, is
indeed something of a
'remedy' after the stream-
ing masses of San Marco.
Try for the front double, the
ceiling of which is graced
with a mid-16th century
fresco by Andrea Medolla.
✉ **Calle di Rimedio,
Castello 4412** ☎ 041
520 62 32; fax 041 521

04 85 🚊 San Zaccaria:
Nos 1, 6, 14, 41, 42, 51,
52, 71, 72, 82 & N

**Locanda San
Barnaba** (3, H5)
This charming new 13
room hotel has been ele-
gantly carved out of a fine
mansion. Rooms are well
equipped and some look
onto the canal. A small terrace graces the top of the
building, as well as a small
canalside garden for breakfast or evening drinks.
✉ **Calle del Traghetto,
Dorsoduro 2785-2786**
☎/fax 041 241 12 33
e info@locanda
-sanbarnaba.com;
www.locanda-san
barnaba.com
🚊 Ca' Rezzonico: No 1
✗ L'Incontro (p. 81)

Locanda Sturion
(3, D10) This guesthouse,
two minutes from the Ponte
di Rialto, has been a hotel
on and off since the 13th
century. It has 11 rooms
loaded with character. The
best are the two generous
ones overlooking the canal.
One downside is the long
stairway up to the hotel.
✉ **Calle del Sturion,
San Polo 679** ☎ 041
523 62 43; fax 041
522 83 78 e info@
locandasturion.com;
www.locandasturion
.com 🚊 San Silvestro:
No 1

Closing Time
Be aware that some
hotels close for part of
the winter. Those on the
Lido are especially prone
to shutting their doors
for as long as Nov-Apr.

BUDGET

Albergo Antico Capon (3, G4)

This place is right on the liveliest square in Dorsoduro and has a variety of bright and airy rooms. The beds are wide and firm.

✉ Campo Santa Margherita, Dorsoduro 3004/b ☎/fax 041 528 52 92 e hotelanticocapon@ hotmail.com 🚊 Ca' Rezzonico: No 1 ✕

Hotel ai do Mori

(3, F13) This hotel is just off St Mark's Square. It has pleasant rooms, some with views of the basilica. The best room is the cosy little double at the top that comes with a terrace attached. The hotel also offers accommodation for groups of three, four and five.

✉ Calle Larga San Marco 658 ☎ 041 520 48 17; fax 041 520 53 28 e www.hotelaidomori .it 🚊 San Zaccaria: Nos 1, 6, 14, 41, 42, 51, 52, 71, 72, 82 & N

Hotel dalla Mora

(3, E3) This hotel is on a small canal near the Casa Peron. It has clean, airy rooms, some (such as No 5) with lovely canal views, and there is a terrace. Bookings are a must.

✉ off Salizzada San Pantalon, Santa Croce 42/a ☎ 041 71 07 03; fax 041 72 30 06 🚊 Ferrovia: Nos 1, 3, 4, 41, 42, 51, 52, 71, 72, 82 & N; Piazzale Roma: Nos 1, 4, 41, 42, 51, 52, 61, 62, 71, 72, 82 & N

Hotel Doni (3, G15)

A stone's throw east of San Marco is this delightful little establishment in an 18th century mansion (although they say the ground floor is 200 years older still). It has been a hotel for more than a century. The 12 rooms are mostly spacious if a little spartan and in one the ceiling is adorned with a fine fresco dating from 1850.

✉ Fondamenta del Vin, Castello 4656 ☎/fax 041 522 42 67 🚊 San Zaccaria: Nos 1, 6, 14, 41, 42, 51, 52, 71, 72, 82 & N

Hotel Galleria (3, K7)

The Hotel Galleria is the only one star hotel right on the Grand Canal, near the Ponte dell'Accademia. The place was an old private mansion before being converted into the modest and warm-feeling hotel it is now. Space is a little tight, but the decor is welcoming. If you can get one of the rooms on the canal, how can you possibly complain?

✉ Rio Terrà Antonio Foscarini, Dorsoduro 878/a ☎/fax 041 520 41 72 e galleria@tin.it; www.hotelgalleria.it 🚊 Accademia: Nos 1, 3, 4, 82 & N

Locanda Casa Petrarca (3, G11)

The Casa Petrarca is one of the nicest budget places to stay in the San Marco area. Breakfast costs extra (€5). It's a bit of a family affair and the cheerful owner speaks English. Rooms are simple but well kept.

✉ Calle Schiavone, San Marco 4386 ☎/fax 041 520 04 30 🚊 Vallaresso & San Marco: Nos 1, 3, 4, 82 & N

Locanda Fiorita (3, G8)

Set on a wonderful little square a spit away from the broad Campo San-to Stefano, the Locanda Fiorita is a gem. The rooms, some of which look onto the square, are simple but well maintained and it is hard to complain about the prices. With its greenery and homey feel, it is a good find. They set up a few breakfast tables outside.

✉ Campiello Nuovo, San Marco 3457/a ☎ 041 523 47 54; fax 041 522 80 43 e locafior@tin.it; www.locandafiorita.com 🚊 San Samuele: Nos 1, 3, 4, 82 & N

Pensione Guerrato

(3, C10) Set amid the Rialto markets, this pensione is a find and one of only two one-star places to have rooms with at least glimpses of the Grand Canal. It is housed in a former convent, which before (so it is said) had served as a hostel for knights heading off on the Third Crusade. It is usually booked pretty solid.

✉ Ruga due Mori, San Polo 240/a ☎ 041 522 71 31; fax 041 528 59 27 e hguerrat@tin.it; web.tiscalinet.it /pensioneguerrato 🚊 Rialto: Nos 1, 4, 82 & N ✕ Cantina Do Mori (p. 82)

No Credit

Many budget hotels in Venice do not accept credit cards so check payment terms when you book.

facts for the visitor

All aboard! Contend with the crowds on Venice's lagoon transport.

ARRIVAL & DEPARTURE

You can get direct flights to Venice from cities across Europe, as well as from New York. There are flights from other parts of Italy, but they can be expensive and generally involve a change in Rome.

Air

Most flights arrive at Marco Polo Airport at Tessera (5, A7), 12km away from the city on the mainland. A handful of flights arrive at Treviso's San Giuseppe Airport, 30km north of Venice.

Marco Polo Airport
Left Luggage
The *deposito* (left luggage) is in the arrivals hall and opens 6am-9pm (€1.80 per item per day).

Information
General Enquiries & Flight Information
☎ 041 260 92 60

Car Park Information
☎ 041 541 59 13

Airport Access
Bus ATVO buses (☎ 041 520 55 30) run to Piazzale Roma (2, F4) via Mestre train station from the airport. The trip takes 20mins and costs €2.60 (€2.10 to/from Mestre). Departures are regular (about 30 daily) from 8.30am to 12.30am. ACTV city bus No 5 also serves the airport from Piazzale Roma (€0.80). It makes more stops and takes closer to 30mins. The first departure from the airport is at 4.08am and services from Piazzale Roma are roughly every 30mins (4.40-12.40am).

Boat The Alilaguna hydrofoil from the airport costs €9.85 to Venice or the Lido and €4.65 to Murano. Pick it up at the Zattere (2, H6) or in front of the Giardini ex Reali (3, H13).

Water Taxi The official rate for the ride between the airport and Piazzetta di San Marco is €44.95. To/from the Lido costs €55.30.

Taxi Just as efficient as the waterborne version, if more prosaic, are taxis with wheels. Expect to pay €25.85 from the airport to Piazzale Roma – a trip of around 15mins.

San Giuseppe Airport
Information
General Enquiries & Flight Information
☎ 0422 31 53 31

Airport Access
Bus The Eurobus service connects with Ryanair flights from London and Brussels. The trip to/from Piazzale Roma takes 1hr 5mins (€4.15). If you are arriving by charter flight, check with the company whether a bus will meet the flight.

Train If your luck is out and no bus for Venice appears, you can catch local bus No 6 from outside the terminal gates which goes to the main train station in Treviso. From there you can proceed to Venice by rail.

Taxi A taxi to Piazzale Roma can take an hour (€62).

Car Parking is provided about 300m south of the airport – follow the signs.

Bus

Although it is possible to reach Venice by bus from some other cities in Italy, it is generally preferable to travel by rail. Eurolines (Agenzia Brusutti), Piazzale Roma 497/e (2, F4; ☎ 041 522 97 73; e www.eurolines.com), is the main carrier for European destinations. Buses depart from Piazzale Roma (2, F4).

Train

Venice is easily reached by train from most Italian destinations, including Bologna, Florence, Milan and Rome. Trenitalia (☎ 848 88 80 88 Italian only; e www.fsonline .com) operates services ranging from slow Regionale and Inter-Regionale trains to faster, limited stops InterCity and Eurostar Italia trains.

Direct international trains run to Venice from Geneva, Munich and Vienna. Otherwise you'll generally need to change trains, often in Milan. It's wise (and sometimes compulsory) to book for international trips and Eurostar trains.

Trains stop in Venice at Stazione di Santa Lucia (3, B1) and at Mestre (5, B2), on the mainland. Tickets (1st and 2nd class) can be bought at stations (from machines and at windows) or from most travel agencies. For credit-card bookings call ☎ 199 16 61 77. Left luggage is opposite platform 14 (€2.60/piece for 12hrs).

From London you can get the Orient Express (☎ 020-7805 5100, e www.orientexpresstrains.com) for a special way to travel to Venice.

Boat

Ferries run year round from Greece to Venice. In Venice you can contact Minoan Lines (☎ 041 271 23 45) or Strintzis Lines (☎ 041 277 05 59) at the passenger port (Stazione Marittima; 2, H4).

Travel Documents

Passport

If you need a visa for Italy, your passport must be valid for several months after the date of entry. EU citizens only need to pack a passport or national ID card.

Visa

Nationals of Australia, Canada, Japan, New Zealand and the USA don't need a visa if entering as tourists for up to three months. Other nationals and those wishing to stay for longer periods or for work or study may need a visa and should check with their local Italian mission.

Customs

Any goods over the duty free limit must be declared. There are no limits on the importation of euros.

Duty Free

Travellers arriving in Italy from non-EU countries can import 200 cigarettes, 1L spirits, 2L wine, 60mL perfume, 250mL eau de toilette, and other goods up to a total of €175.50; anything in excess must be declared and duty paid. People travelling within the EU can import VAT-free goods (on sale at European airports).

GETTING AROUND

Walking is the best way to get to know the city, but there are other options. The Azienda Consorzio Trasporti Veneziano (ACTV; ☎ 041 528 78 86; e www.actv.it) runs public transport in the Venice area. It runs the water bus (vaporetto) network in Venice, and the buses that connect the lagoon city with Mestre and other mainland areas. Transport information (among other things) is available from ACTV's subsidiary, Vela, on ☎ 899 90 90 90. Water taxis are the other option.

Wheeled taxis run from Piazzale Roma to the mainland.

Travel Passes

Those planning to use the *vaporetti* even moderately are advised to buy a *biglietto a tempo*, a ticket valid on all transport (except the Alilaguna, Clodia and LineaBlù services). Valid for 24hrs from the first validation, they cost €9.30 or €23.25/31/38.75 for three/four/five people. *Biglietto tre giorni*, a three day version, costs €18.10 (€12.95 with a Rolling Venice pass; see Discounts p. 115). A weekly pass *(biglietto sette giorni)* costs €31. Buy passes at ACTV and Vela outlets and some tobacconists *(tabacchi)* and newsstands *(edicole)*.

Vaporetto

Several vaporetto (water bus) lines run up and down the Grand Canal, although some are *limitato* (limited-stops services). You can generally be sure that all will stop at St Mark's, Accademia, Rialto, Ferrovia (for the train station) and Piazzale Roma. Line No 1 is an all stops job that takes a little over 30mins to meander between Ferrovia and St Mark's.

Some services continue to the Lido, while others circle around the southern side of Venice and serve stops along Giudecca island. Yet more leave the main northern Venice stop of Fondamente Nuove for Murano, Burano and Torcello.

Tickets must be bought in advance and validated prior to boarding. Single-trip tickets cost €3.10 (return €5.20) – so transport passes make good sense. Booklets with network maps and timetables are sometimes available from ACTV offices. Timetables are also listed at stops. Some lines stop operating by as early as 9pm. A night (N) vaporetto runs along the Grand Canal and also serves the Lido and Giudecca.

Getting the vaporetto can be confusing. You may have the right number but be going the wrong way. The San Marco–San Zaccaria area quays and those at Piazzale Roma and Ferrovia can be confusing too, as departure quays vary widely according to line and destination.

Traghetto

The *traghetto* is a commuter gondola that crosses the Grand Canal at strategic spots and saves on a lot of shoe leather. Some operate from around 9am to 6pm, while others stop at around midday. A crossing costs €0.40 and passengers stand – quite a balance test for newbies!

Water Taxi

Water taxis (motorboats) are costly, with a set €13.95 charge for the first 7mins, plus €0.30/15secs thereafter. On top come surcharges: €4.15 to book by phone ; €4.40 10pm-7am; €4.65 on holidays; €1.15/piece of luggage; and €1.60/extra head if more than four people are travelling. You can find water taxis at stands along the Grand Canal or call ☎ 041 522 12 65, ☎ 041 71 61 24 or ☎ 041 522 23 03.

Bus

Regular buses (including a night service) run from Piazzale Roma to Mestre (outside the train station) and other mainland destinations. Tickets cost €0.80 (or €7.25/10) and must be bought at newsstands or tobacconists prior to boarding and validated on board.

Train

All trains leaving Stazione di Santa Lucia stop in Mestre. Tickets (available from newsstands at the train station) cost €0.95 on the slower

trains. The last trains run around midnight – check timetables posted at either train station.

Taxi

If you need a land taxi to the airport or anywhere between Venice and Mestre, you can pick one up from the rank in Piazzale Roma or call ☎ 041 523 77 74 or 041 93 62 22.

Car & Motorcycle

Clearly you cannot drive anywhere in Venice. If you wish, you can pay exorbitant rates (up to €24.80/24hrs) to park in one of several car parks around Piazzale Roma or Tronchetto. It is cheaper (as little as €4.15/day) to opt for one of the car parks opposite the train station at Mestre.

Road Rules

Should you decide to go on driving tours outside Venice, bear in mind that Italians drive on the right and that the wearing of seat belts is compulsory. In built-up areas the speed limit is 50km/hr; it scales up to 130km/hr on motorways. The blood-alcohol limit when driving is 0.08%.

Rental

You may want a car for excursions beyond Venice (although you can live without one). Expect to pay around €62/day, less at weekends. Avis has an office in Piazzale Roma (Italy-wide ☎ 199 10 01 33), as do Europcar (toll free ☎ 800 82 80 50), Hertz (Italy-wide ☎ 199 11 22 11) and Expressway (☎ 041 522 30 00). They all have reps at Marco Polo Airport too.

Driving Licence & Permit

Bring with you either an EU driving licence or an International Driving Permit plus your home country licence.

Motoring Organisations

The Automobile Club Italiano (ACI) provides free emergency roadside assistance (☎ 116) once only to members of foreign automobile associations to get you and the car to the nearest ACI registered mechanic. The cost for nonmembers is €82.70.

A European breakdown assistance policy, such as those available from the AA or RAC, is a worthwhile investment.

PRACTICAL INFORMATION

Climate & When to Go

It's almost always high season in Venice, although the city is busiest in spring (Easter-June) and Sept-Oct. Accommodation can be hard to find then, as well as around Christmas-New Year and Carnevale period (Feb). July-Aug tend to be oppressively hot and humid (and many places close for the August holidays), while winters can be grey and wet, with flooding a frequent occurrence in Nov-Dec. Venice is at its sparkling best beneath a crystal blue sky in early spring, while some find the mists of early winter (if and when they strike) enchanting.

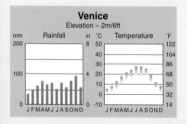

Tourist Information

Tourist Information Abroad

Information on Venice is available from these branches of the Italian State Tourist Office (☎ www.enit.it):

Australia
L26, 44 Market St, Sydney 2000 (☎ 02-9262 1666, ☎ enitour@ihug.com.au)

Canada
Suite 907, S Tower, 17 Bloor St E, Toronto, Ontario M4W3R8 (☎ 416-925 4882, ☎ enit.canada@on.aibn.com)

UK
1 Princess St, London W1R 9AY (☎ 020-7355 1557, ☎ enitlond@globalnet.co.uk)

USA
630 Fifth Ave, Suite 1565, New York, NY 10111 (☎ 212-245 4822, ☎ enitny@italiantourism.com)

Local Tourist Information

Azienda di Promozione Turistica (APT) services Venice and the province. There's an information service too (☎ 041 529 87 11, fax 041 523 03 99).

The main APT office is at Piazza San Marco 71/f (3, H12; Mon-Sat 9.45am-3.15pm). Another office, or Infopoint, operates in the Venice Pavilion (3, J12; 9am-6pm). There are further APT offices at the train station (3, A2; 8am-8pm) and in Piazzale Roma (2, E4; 9am-6pm).

Embassies & Consulates

Most countries have embassies in Rome and a few are represented by consulates in Venice. Where there is no representation in Venice, the nearest available embassy or consulate is listed:

Australia
Via Borgogna 2, Milan (☎ 02 77 70 41)

Canada
Riviera Ruzzante 25, Padua (☎ 049 878 11 47)

New Zealand
Via Zara 28, Rome (☎ 06 441 71 71)

South Africa
Via Tanaro 14, Rome (☎ 06 85 25 11)

UK
Palazzo Querini, Dorsoduro 1051 (3, J6; ☎ 041 522 72 07)

USA
Largo Donegani 1, Milan (☎ 02 29 03 51)

Money

Currency

From 1 January 2002 Italy became one of 12 EU states to adopt the euro as its official currency, with the lira withdrawn from 1 March. The prices in this book are conversions from lire and may change slightly.

There are seven euro notes, each a different colour and size, and they come in denominations of €500, €200, €100, €50, €20, €10 and €5. The eight euro coins are in denominations of €2 and €1, then 50, 20, 10, five, two and one cents.

Travellers Cheques

Travellers cheques can be cashed at any bank or exchange office (watch commissions). American Express (AmEx), Salizzada San Moisè, San Marco 1471 (3, H11; ☎ 041 520 08 44) opens Mon-Fri 9am-5.30pm and Sat 9am-12.30pm. Thomas Cook, Piazza San Marco 142 (3, G13; ☎ 041 522 47 51), and Riva del Ferro 5126 (3, D11; ☎ 041 528 73 58) open Mon-Sat 8.45am-8pm and Sun 9am-6pm.

Credit Cards

Visa and MasterCard are the most widely accepted cards in Italy. Small hotels and restaurants sometimes don't accept cards. For 24hr card cancellations or assistance, call:

AmEx	☎ 800 87 43 33
Diners Club	☎ 800 86 40 64
MasterCard	☎ 800 87 08 66
Visa	☎ 800 87 72 32

ATMs

Automatic Teller Machines (ATMs) are most easily found at the train station, in busy squares and streets (especially Lista di Spagna and Strada Nova linking the station and St Mark's Square). Visa and MasterCard in particular are widely accepted.

Changing Money

Banks generally offer the fairest rates and lowest commissions. The latter can vary from a fixed fee of €1.50 to a percentage. *Cambi* (bureaux de change) tend to impose heftier commissions of 10% plus!

Banks are generally open Mon-Fri 8.30am-1.30pm and 3.30-4.30pm. Some main branches also open Sat 9am-12.30pm. Hours tend to vary a little from bank to bank. Bureaux de change tend to open Mon-Sat 8am-8pm. Some open on Sunday.

Tipping

In restaurants where service is not included it's customary to leave a 10% tip; if service is included you can leave a little extra if you feel it's warranted. In bars Italians often leave small change. Tipping taxi drivers is not common practice, but you should tip the porter at upmarket hotels (about €0.50/bag).

Discounts

Admission to all state museums is free for EU citizens under 18 and over 65. Otherwise there are precious few reductions for sights (always ask, just in case!) and none (except for students resident in Venice) for public transport.

Student & Youth Cards

Possession of the International Student Identity Card (ISIC) may get you reduced admission to some sights, but often it will not. Ask but don't expect frequent joy.

Those aged 14 to 29 can obtain a Rolling Venice card (€2.60), offering significant traveller discounts, from the Assessorato alla Gioventù, Corte Contarina 1529 (3, H11; ☎ 041 274 76 50; fax 041 274 76 42). It can also be obtained from AIG, Calle del Castelforte 3101, San Polo (3, E4; ☎ 041 520 44 14); Agenzia Arte e Storia, Corte Canal 659, Santa Croce (3, C3; ☎ 041 524 02 32); the ACTV in Calle dei Fuseri, San Marco (3, G11); and some Vela outlets.

Travel Insurance

A policy covering theft, loss, medical expenses and compensation for cancellation or delays in your travel arrangements is highly recommended. If items are lost or stolen, make sure you get a police report straight away – otherwise your insurer might not pay up.

Opening Hours

Public offices tend to open Mon-Fri from 8.30am to around 2pm. Regular business hours are generally Mon-Fri 8.30am-1.30pm and 4-7.30pm. Much the same can be said of shops, although a lot depends on the whim of the shopkeepers. The few larger stores tend to open through lunch as well. Many stores open on Saturday and some directed mainly at tourists open on Sunday too.

Restaurants generally open 12.30-3pm (with kitchens mostly closed by 2pm) for lunch and 7.30-11.30pm (kitchens closed by 10.30pm) for dinner. Most take one day off in the week.

Public Holidays

Jan 1	New Year's Day
Jan 6	Epiphany
Mar/Apr	Good Friday

Mar/Apr	Easter Monday
Apr 25	Liberation Day
May 1	Labour Day
Aug 15	Feast of the Assumption
Nov 1	All Saints Day
Dec 8	Feast of the Immaculate Conception
Dec 25	Christmas Day
Dec 26	Boxing Day

Time

Venice Standard Time is 1hr ahead of GMT/UTC. Daylight savings is practised from the last Sunday in March to the last Sunday in October. At noon in Venice it's:

6am in New York
3am in Los Angeles
11am in London
1pm in Johannesburg
11pm in Auckland
9pm in Sydney

Electricity

The electric current in Venice is 220V, 50Hz, and plugs have two round pins, as in the rest of continental Europe. Bring international plug adaptors for your appliances. North Americans need a voltage converter (although top hotels have provision for 110V appliances).

Weights & Measures

The metric system is standard, and like other continental Europeans, Italians use commas in decimals and points to indicate thousands. See the conversion table on p. 122.

Post

Italy's postal service is notoriously unreliable but it is improving. The main post office, Salizzada del Fondaco dei Tedeschi (3, D12; Mon-Sat 8.10am-7pm), is just near the Ponte di Rialto. You can buy stamps here or at tobacconists (look for the *tabacchi* sign).

Postal Rates

Postcards and letters up to 20g sent priority post *(posta prioritaria)* cost €0.78 to the Americas, Australia and New Zealand and €0.62 within Italy and Europe and to Mediterranean countries.

Telephone

A local phone call from a public phone will cost €0.20 for 3-6mins, depending on the time of day. Orange phone booths of the national phone company, Telecom Italia, are spread across the city, especially in busy areas such as the train station, near the main post office and along main thoroughfares. Most take coins and all take Telecom phonecards.

Phonecards

Telecom Italia phonecards are available in €2.60-25.85 denominations from post offices, tobacconists and some newsstands. They can be used for local and international calls. Some Internet centres provide cut-rate international call facilities.

Lonely Planet's eKno Communication Card, specifically aimed at travellers, provides competitive international calls (avoid using it for local calls), messaging services and free email. Log on to [e] www.ekno.lonelyplanet.com for service information.

Mobile Phones

Italy uses the GSM cellular phone system, compatible with phones sold in the rest of Europe, Australia and most of Asia, but not those from North America and Japan. Check with your service provider that they have a roaming agreement with a local counterpart. Making and receiving calls with your home mobile phone in Italy can be extremely costly.

Country & City Codes

The city code (including the 0) is an integral part of the number and must be dialled, whether calling from next door or abroad; mobile numbers have no initial 0. The codes are:

Italy	☎ 39
Venice	☎ 041

Useful Numbers

Local Directory Enquiries	☎ 12
International Directory Enquiries	☎ 176
International Operator	☎ 170
Reverse-Charge (collect; see also County Direct below)	☎ 170

International Direct Dial Codes

Dial ☎ 00 followed by:

Australia	☎ 61
Canada	☎ 1
Japan	☎ 81
New Zealand	☎ 64
South Africa	☎ 27
UK	☎ 44
USA	☎ 1

Country Direct

An easier (and often cheaper) way to make reverse-charge calls is to dial Country Direct. You dial a special number that includes your country code (eg, Australia 172-10-61, UK (BT) 172-00-44, USA (AT&T) 172-11-11). Check the codes with your phone company before leaving home, or in the introductory pages of Telecom Italia White Pages.

Digital Resources

Venice has taken a while to catch on to the Internet craze but cybercafes (mostly aimed at computerless visitors) began to mushroom in early 2000. Access generally costs €5.20-8.30/hr.

Internet Service Providers

Most global ISPs have dial-in nodes in Italy – download a list of them before you leave home. Otherwise you can open an account with a local ISP (if you have your own computer) or rely on Internet cafes.

Internet Cafes

EasyContact
Campo Nazario Sauro 1005/a, Santa Croce (3, B5; ☎ 041 71 10 97; e www.easy -contact.it; 9am-7pm; €7.25/hr)

The Netgate
Calle dei Preti Crosera 3812a, Dorsoduro (3, F4; ☎ 041 244 02 13; e www.the netgate.it; Mon-Fri 10.15am-8pm, Sat 10.15am-10pm, Sun 2.15-10pm; €5.20/hr)

Net House
Campo Santo Stefano 2958-2967, San Marco (3, H8; ☎ 041 277 11 90; 24hrs, they claim!; minimum €2.60 for the first 20mins and €0.13/min thereafter)

Omniservice Internet Café
Fondamenta dei Tolentini 220, Santa Croce (3, C2; ☎ 041 71 04 70; 8am-10pm; €5.20/hr)

Useful Sites

The Lonely Planet Web site (e www .lonelyplanet.com) offers a speedy link to many of Venice's Web sites. Others to try include:

ENIT (Italian State Tourist Board)
e www.enit.it/uk

Ombra.Net
e www.ombra.net

Venice Banana
e www.venicebanana.com

VeNETia
e www.comune.venezia.it

Venezia Net
e www.doge.it

Doing Business

If you wish to do business in Venice contact your own country's trade department (such as the DTI in the UK). The commercial department of the Italian embassy in your own country should also have information – at least on red tape. In Italy,

the trade office of your embassy can provide tips and contacts.

Venezia Congressi, Campiello Gambara, Dorsoduro 1056 (3, J6; ☎ 041 522 84 00; fax 041 523 89 95), and ENDAR (aka Veneto Congressi), Fondamenta dell'Osmarin, Castello 4966 (2, F10; ☎ 041 523 85 60), should be able to help with the organisation of business conventions in Venice.

Newspapers & Magazines

Major Italian dailies include *Corriere della Sera* and *La Repubblica*. The local dailies are *Il Gazzettino* and *Nuova Venezia*. A raft of European newspapers and news magazines, along with the *International Herald Tribune* and *USA Today*, are available at main newsstands in key points of the city, such as the train station and near Ponte di Rialto and St Mark's Square. A handy local publication for information on what's on in Venice is *Venezia News*, a monthly magazine in Italian and English.

Radio

There are three state-owned stations: RAI-1 (1332AM or 89.7FM), RAI-2 (846AM or 91.7FM) and RAI-3 (93.7FM). They offer a combination of classical and light music with news broadcasts and discussion programmes. Among the better local commercial stations is Radio Venezia (101.1FM), with news and, on balance, not a bad selection of music.

You can pick up BBC World Service on medium wave at 648 kHz, on short wave at 6.195MHz, 9.410MHz, 12.095MHz and 15.575 MHz, and on long wave at 198kHz, depending on where you are and the time of day.

TV

The three state-run stations, RAI-1, RAI-2 and RAI-3, compete with the private Canale 5, Italia 1, Rete 4 and La 7 stations, to provide a remarkable diet of talk and variety shows and the occasional decent programme (especially on RAI-3). Several local stations also contribute to the generally appalling small screen diet. Many of the better hotels receive BBC World, CNN, Sky Channel and others.

Photography & Video

Print and slide film are readily available from stores around the city, but only a few shops sell camera gear and do repairs.

Italy uses the PAL video system (the same as in Australia and most of Europe). This system is not compatible with NTSC (used in North America, Japan and Latin America) or Secam (used in France and Germany) unless the machine is multisystem.

Health

Immunisations
There are no vaccination requirements for entering Italy.

Precautions
Venice's tap water is safe to drink (although many people prefer the bottled stuff) and food preparation is fairly hygienic (Italians are fussy about food). Heat and humidity might be a problem in summer – wear a hat and loose, comfortable clothing and drink plenty of fluids.

Insurance & Medical Treatment
Travel insurance is advisable to cover any medical treatment you may need while away. All foreigners can seek emergency medical

treatment in public hospitals or clinics. EU citizens (present the E111 form) and Australians (show your Medicare card) have the right to the full range of public health services. If you end up in a private clinic, you'll have to pay.

The level of care in hospitals in Venice and on the mainland is reasonable, but the Italian public health system is fairly oversubscribed.

Medical Services
Hospitals with 24hr accident and emergency departments include:

Ospedale Civile
 Campo SS Giovanni e Paolo, Castello 5666 (3, B15; ☎ 041 529 41 11)
Ospedale Umberto I
 Via Circonvallazione 50, Mestre (5, A3; ☎ 041 260 71 11)

Dental Services
If you chip a tooth or require emergency treatment, head to the Ambulatorio Odontostomatologico at the Ospedale Civile (see above).

Pharmacies
Pharmacies *(farmacie)* are usually open 9am-12.30pm and 3.30-7.30pm. Most are closed on Saturday afternoon and Sunday. When closed, pharmacies display a list of other ones that are open. Information on all-night pharmacies is listed in *Un Ospite di Venezia*, a free booklet available at tourist offices and some hotels.

Toilets

Stopping at a bar for a coffee and a trip to the loo is the common solution to those sudden awkward urges. Otherwise, public toilets (visitors pay €0.52, residents €0.25) are scattered about Venice – look for the 'WC Toilette' signs. They are generally open 7am-7pm.

Safety Concerns

Venice is by and large a safe and tame city. Tourists are, however, frequently targeted by pickpockets, especially in crowded areas such as St Mark's Square, around the Rialto and on vaporetti. Theft from foreign and hire cars has been reported at some car parks. Ignore all approaches from boat captains or illegal 'taxis' that prey on those tourists arriving on Tronchetto island (where they park their cars; 2, D1). There is no need for water taxis anywhere as regular vaporetti call here. Violence is rare and the city is quiet at night.

Lost Property
For items lost on buses or vaporetti call ☎ 041 272 21 79, or on the train ☎ 041 78 52 38. Otherwise, call the local police *(vigili urbani)* on ☎ 041 522 45 76. Their lost property office is at Piazzale Roma.

Keeping Copies
Make photocopies of all your important documents, keep some with you, separate from the originals, and leave a copy at home. You can also store details of documents in Lonely Planet's free online Travel Vault, password-protected and accessible worldwide. See [e] www .ekno.lonelyplanet.com.

Emergency Numbers

Ambulance	☎ 118
Fire	☎ 115
Police	☎ 113
Police (non-emergency)	☎ 041 271 57 72
Carabinieri (military police)	☎ 112
Rape Crisis Line	☎ 041 534 92 15

Women Travellers

Of the main destinations in Italy, Venice has to be the safest for women. The kind of bravado that

has more southerly Italians trying it on insistently with foreign women seems largely absent here. If you do get unwanted attention, whatever methods you use to deal with it at home should work here.

Tampons (and more commonly sanitary towels) are available in pharmacies and supermarkets. Prescriptions are needed for the contraceptive pill.

Gay & Lesbian Travellers

Homosexuality is legal in Italy and well tolerated in Venice and the north in general. The legal age of consent is 16. However, overt displays of affection by homosexual couples could attract a negative response.

In Venice there's little in the way of a gay scene, with no clearly gay establishments.

Information & Organisations

Even getting information is a trifle difficult. The local gay association, ArciGay Dedalo, Via Costa 38a, Mestre (5, A2; ☎ 041 753 84 15), is secreted away on the mainland.

Senior Travellers

Plenty of seniors visit Venice, but remember that the unique nature of the place means you will do a lot of walking, especially up and down the many bridges that cross the city's canals. Not all hotels have lifts so check this before booking.

Disabled Travellers

Venice is clearly not a dream location for the disabled, but they have not been left out completely. The city map available from APT offices has areas of the city shaded in yellow to indicate that they can be negotiated without running into a bridge. Some of the bridges are equipped with lifts *(montascale)* that are marked on the maps. You can get hold of a key to operate these lifts from the tourist offices.

Most of the important vaporetto lines allow wheelchair access. Those that don't are Nos 13, 20 and 51/52. There are six bus lines adapted for wheelchair-users, including No 2 (Piazzale Roma–Mestre train station).

Slight modifications have been made to some of the city's sights to facilitate access to those in wheelchairs, but there is a long way to go.

Information & Organisations

The Rome-based Consorzio Cooperative Integrate (CO.IN), Via Enrico Giglioli 54/a, Rome (☎ 06 712 90 11; Mon-Fri 9am-5pm; |e| turismo@coinsociale.it; www .coinsociale.it), is the best point of reference for disabled travellers in Italy, although it concentrates on the capital. In Venice you can try Informahandicap, Villa Franchin, Via Garibaldi 155, Mestre (5, A2; ☎ 041 534 17 00; |e| informahandicap@comune.venezia.it).

Language

The Venetians speak with an oddly staccato accent, which Italians farther south have a habit of poking fun at. True-blue Venetians actually speak a dialect (for some a separate language), known commonly as Venessian. Although clearly similar, it contains many different words and Italian speakers will be surprised at how hard to understand it can be!

Many locals speak at least some English, exposed as they are to the constant influx of foreigners. Still, any attempt to speak Italian will be appreciated. Here are some useful phrases to get you started. Grab a copy of Lonely Planet's *Italian phrasebook* if you'd like to know more.

Basics

Hello.	*Buongiorno.* (pol)
	Ciao. (inf)
Goodbye.	*Arrivederci.* (pol)
	Ciao. (inf)
Yes.	*Sì.*
No.	*No.*
Please.	*Per favore/*
	Per piacere.
Thank you.	*Grazie.*
You're welcome.	*Prego.*
Excuse me.	*Mi scusi.*
Sorry. (forgive me)	*Mi perdoni.*
Do you speak English?	*Parla inglese?*
I don't understand.	*Non capisco.*
How much is it?	*Quanto costa?*

Getting Around

When does the ... leave/arrive?	*A che ora parte/arriva ... ?*
bus	*l'autobus*
boat	*la barca*
train	*il treno*
I'd like a ... ticket	*Vorrei un biglietto di ...*
one-way	*solo andata*
return	*andata e ritorno*
Where is ... ?	*Dov'è ... ?*
Go straight ahead.	*Si va sempre diritto.*
Turn left/right.	*Giri a sinistra/ destra.*

Around Town

I'm looking for ...	*Cerco ...*
the market	*il mercato*
a public toilet	*un gabinetto*
the tourist office	*l'ufficio di turismo*
What time does it open/close?	*A che ora (si) apre/chiude?*

Accommodation

a hotel	*un albergo*
Do you have any rooms available?	*Avete delle camere libere?*
a ... room	*una camera ...*
single	*singola*
twin	*doppia*
double	*matrimoniale*
a room with bathroom	*una camera con bagno*

Eating

breakfast	*prima colazione*
lunch	*pranzo*
dinner	*cena*
The bill, please.	*Il conto, per favore.*

Shopping

I'm just looking.	*Sto solo guardando.*
How much is it?	*Quanto costa?*
Do you accept...?	*Accettate...?*
credit cards	*carte di credito*
travellers cheques	*assegni per viaggiatori*

Time, Days & Numbers

What time is it?	*Che ora è?*
today	*oggi*
tomorrow	*domani*
yesterday	*ieri*
morning	*mattina*
afternoon	*pomeriggio*
day	*giorno*
Monday	*lunedì*
Tuesday	*martedì*
Wednesday	*mercoledì*
Thursday	*giovedì*
Friday	*venerdì*
Saturday	*sabato*
Sunday	*domenica*

1	uno
2	due
3	tre
4	quattro
5	cinque
6	sei
7	sette
8	otto
9	nove
10	dieci
100	cento
1000	mille

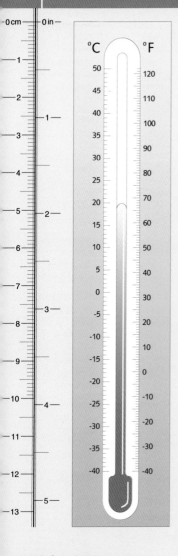

Conversion Table

Clothing Sizes
Measurements approximate only; try before you buy.

Women's Clothing

Aust/NZ	8	10	12	14	16	18
Europe	36	38	40	42	44	46
Japan	5	7	9	11	13	15
UK	8	10	12	14	16	18
USA	6	8	10	12	14	16

Women's Shoes

Aust/NZ	5	6	7	8	9	10
Europe	35	36	37	38	39	40
France only	35	36	38	39	40	42
Japan	22	23	24	25	26	27
UK	3½	4½	5½	6½	7½	8½
USA	5	6	7	8	9	10

Men's Clothing

Aust/NZ	92	96	100	104	108	112
Europe	46	48	50	52	54	56
Japan	S		M	M		L
UK	35	36	37	38	39	40
USA	35	36	37	38	39	40

Men's Shirts (Collar Sizes)

Aust/NZ	38	39	40	41	42	43
Europe	38	39	40	41	42	43
Japan	38	39	40	41	42	43
UK	15	15½	16	16½	17	17½
USA	15	15½	16	16½	17	17½

Men's Shoes

Aust/NZ	7	8	9	10	11	12
Europe	41	42	43	44½	46	47
Japan	26	27	27.5	28	29	30
UK	7	8	9	10	11	12
USA	7½	8½	9½	10½	11½	12½

Weights & Measures

Weight
1kg = 2.2lb
1lb = 0.45kg
1g = 0.04oz
1oz = 28g

Volume
1 litre = 0.26 US gallons
1 US gallon = 3.8 litres
1 litre = 0.22 imperial gallons
1 imperial gallon = 4.55 litres

Length & Distance
1 inch = 2.54cm
1cm = 0.39 inches
1m = 3.3ft = 1.1yds
1ft = 0.3m
1km = 0.62 miles
1 mile = 1.6km

lonely planet

Lonely Planet is the world's most successful independent travel information company with offices in Australia, the US, the UK and France. With a reputation for comprehensive, reliable travel information and with over 650 titles and 22 series catering for travellers' individual needs, Lonely Planet is a print and electronic publishing leader.

At Lonely Planet we believe that travellers can make a positive contribution to the countries they visit – if they respect their host communities and spend their money wisely. Since 1986 a percentage of the income from books has been donated to aid and human rights projects.

www.lonelyplanet.com

For news, views and free subscriptions to print and email newsletters plus a full list of LP titles, click on Lonely Planet's award-winning Web site.

On the Town

A romantic escape to Paris or a mad shopping dash through New York City, the locals' secret bars or a city's top attractions – whether you have 24 hours to kill or months to explore, Lonely Planet's On the Town products will give you the low-down.

Condensed guides are ideal pocket guides for when time is tight. Their quick-view maps, full-colour layout and opinionated reviews help short-term visitors target the top sights and discover the very best eating, shopping and entertainment options a city has to offer.

For more in-depth coverage, **city guides** offer insights into a city's character and cultural background as well as providing broad coverage of where to eat, stay and play. **CitySync**, a digital guide for your handheld unit, allows you to reference stacks of opinionated, well researched travel information. Portable and durable **city maps** are perfect for locating those back street bars or hard-to-find local haunts.

'Ideal for a generation of fast movers.'

– *Gourmet Traveller* on Condensed guides

Condensed Guides

- Amsterdam
- Athens
- Bangkok (Sept 2002)
- Barcelona
- Boston
- Chicago
- Dublin
- Frankfurt
- Hong Kong
- London
- Los Angeles (Oct 2002)
- New York City
- Paris
- Prague
- Rome
- San Francisco (Oct 2002)
- Singapore (Oct 2002)
- Sydney
- Tokyo
- Venice
- Washington, DC

index

PLACES TO EAT

PLACES TO STAY

SHOPS

sights – quick index